MW00978233

WHAT'S RIGHT
WHAT'S WRONG
In An
Upside-
Down
World

WHAT'S RIGHT WHAT'S WRONG

In An Upside-Down WORLD

By

FRED HARTLEY

OLIVER NELSON

A DIVISION OF
THOMAS NELSON PUBLISHERS

NASHVILLE

Published in Nashville, Tennessee, by Oliver-Nelson Books, a division
of Thomas Nelson, Inc., Publishers, and distributed in Canada by
Lawson Falle, Ltd., Cambridge, Ontario.

Unless otherwise noted, the Bible version used in this publication is
the HOLY BIBLE: NEW INTERNATIONAL VERSION. Copyright ©
1973, 1978, 1984 by the International Bible Society. Used by
permission of Zondervan Bible Publishers.

Scripture quotations marked NKJV are taken from THE NEW KING
JAMES VERSION. Copyright © 1979, 1980, 1982, Thomas Nelson,
Inc., Publishers.

The quoted material about "Wayne" (chapter 3) is taken from the
Miami Herald, March 1987. The quoted material about "Pedro"
(chapter 11) is taken from the *Miami Herald,* July 1987 and is
reprinted by permission.

The letter to a son from his deceased father (chapter 11) is taken
from Paul L. Tan's *Encyclopedia of Seven Thousand, Seven Hundred
Quotations,* Assurance Publishers, 1979. Reprinted by permission.

The quoted material from Bubba Smith (chapter 13) is taken from
"That Little Voice Just Kept Chanting: 'Stop, Bubba, Stop'" by Scott
Ostler. Copyright, 1986, *Los Angeles Times,* Reprinted by permission.

Most names and events have been fictionalized for protection of
privacy and maintenance of confidentiality.

Printed in the United States of America.

Library of Congress Cataloging-in-Publication Data

Hartley, Fred.
    What's right, what's wrong in an upside-down world / Fred Hartley.
      p. cm.
    ISBN 0-8407-9518-1 (pbk.) : $6.95
    1. Youth—Religious life. 2. Youth—Conduct of life.
  3. Christian life—1960- I. Title.
  BV4531.2.H354 1988
  241'.088055—dc19

                        87–34561
ISBN 0-8407-9518-1   CIP

To the family of
Merle & Ruby Kendall
and to the vision they have
of raising up
many godly generations

Contents

1

A Butterfly in a Blizzard

VALUES are a matter of life and death. In fact, anyone without a value system is like a butterfly in a blizzard. He doesn't stand a chance.

It is June 17, 1986. The place is New York City's Felt Forum. It is the first round of the NBA (National Basketball Association) draft, and Len Bias is the happiest guy in the world. Commissioner David Stern has just called Bias's name over the loud speaker. Someone hands him a green Celtics' hat, and his 6'8", well-muscled body moves toward the podium.

For two years he has been the ACC Player of the Year with an average of 20.9 points a game. He finished as Maryland's all-time leading scorer with 2,149 points. Even rival North Carolina coach Jim Volvano said, "Lenny was almost the perfect basketball player: the body, the quickness, the jumping ability." In his four years at Maryland, he never missed a game due to injury.

This moment he stands in front of dozens of microphones and a screaming crowd with what seems to be nothing but success stretching out in front of him like an endless expressway. Reebok shoe company has agreed to a Bias endorsement that would provide him with financial security for life. Larry Bird is so ecstatic that he even promises to show up at rookie camp since Bias will be there.

There is just one problem: forty hours from now, twenty-two-year-old Lenny Bias will be dead of cardiorespiratory arrest. The state medical examiner will quickly determine that cocaine killed him. The redness in his windpipe and the congestion in his mucous membrane will help determine that Bias freebased cocaine. A high concentration of the drug will be found in his blood—6.5 milligrams per liter. His successful future will have disappeared in a vapor.

Even though he wasn't pushy about his conviction, his friends and family called Bias a card-carrying, born-again Christian. He had a reputation around his teammates for being a straight kid, a non-drug user. But something went terribly wrong. Late that Wednesday night Bias compromised his convictions and decided to forget his reputation. Somehow his values were turned upside down. What he said he would never do was now history. The unthinkable happened. He got stoned. His heart stopped ticking. His friends panicked. They called emergency, but the rescue unit was helpless. It was too late. His life was wasted. Drugs buried another victim. What might have been went down the drain.

Who's to blame?

▸ His teammates and friends who didn't care enough to talk him out of the cocaine?

▸ The creep who gave it to him?

▸ Or Len himself, for exchanging all he had for a cheap, late-night buzz?

One thing for sure, when our values get turned upside down, it's difficult to make right choices. When we lose our sense of balance, everything becomes a blur. Values are a matter of life and death.

EVERYDAY VALUES

The crazy thing about values is that even though they are important, we can cruise through life without even knowing they exist. We grow up, go to school, make friends, and before we realize it, we find ourselves asking questions that never before mattered. The fact is this: Once we become teenagers, we make value judgments everytime we step out the front door.

- Who says it's wrong to smoke marijuana or use cocaine?
- Why do I have to be the only kid in eleventh grade with a ten o'clock curfew?
- Everybody else goes to bed with her boyfriend—why can't I?
- My parents are just too old-fashioned. I can't be expected to do everything they say, can I?
- Isn't it okay to cheat on the exam, as long as I don't get caught?
- What difference does it make if I don't tell the whole truth?
- Why should I be the only one not to laugh at dirty jokes? After all, some of them are pretty funny!
- Church is a drag and full of hypocrites—why bother going?
- What's wrong with getting an abortion?

Isn't it better than an unwanted baby?

We answer these questions according to our value system. It doesn't matter who we are—punk rockers in London or preppies on Long Island—we all have standards by which we judge right and wrong.

DIFFERENT VALUES

Values are invisible. That's why many people never recognize their existence. But once we recognize what they are, it sure makes them much easier to handle.

There are different kinds of values:

▸ *Financial values* tell us how much a product is worth. We know it would be stupid to buy a piece of bubble gum for ten dollars. We also know we can't expect to pay twenty-five cents for a skateboard. It is important to understand financial values to keep from getting ripped off.

▸ *Social values* tell us how to act in public. (Some people call them *manners*.) Even though they can be boring, it's important for us to know things like covering our mouth when we sneeze and not spitting into the wind. How would you feel if the kid sitting across from you in the cafeteria coughed without covering his mouth right after he bit into his egg-salad sandwich? Gross! Social values are important to keep us from being embarrassed or objectionable.

▸ *Moral values* tell us what is right and wrong. They help us make decisions about sex, drugs, alcohol, parents, grades, work, dating, marriage, college, career, and more. Of all the different varieties of values, these are by far the most important. They protect us from losing self-respect and dignity. Moral values are what this book is all about.

INVISIBLE WALLS

Part of maturing, besides growing hair under our arms, is learning to identify values and deciding which values are worth living for. Hair grows naturally—whether we want it to or not. But unfortunately, values don't come as easily. In fact, it is not uncommon for people to get old and gray without ever choosing their value system.

Values are invisible, like invisible walls. At times we walk into them and bruise ourselves before we realize it. At other times we walk through them without even knowing it, and the scars won't show up until later. Even though values are invisible, we need to get to know them in order to save ourselves a lot of aches and pains.

Choosing our own moral values is an essential part of growing up. Yes, it is painful and tiring and frustrating. No, everyone will not agree with our conclusions. But the only other option is to throw our values in a dumpster altogether—in which case, we might as well climb in with them.

"WEIRDO"

Often we don't wake up and realize the importance of values until we are under pressure, until someone grabs us around the neck and screams,

"Hey, Weirdo! What's your problem?" I didn't know what values were until seventh grade.

I often watched horror movies with my best friend Howard on Saturday nights. We saw *The Return of Frankenstein, The Loch Ness Monster, The Ape Man and Godzilla,* and other thrillers. We would pop popcorn and laugh our socks off at those stupid movies.

One night during a commercial, he ran to the door to be sure his mother wasn't listening, turned to me with this weird look in his eye and asked, "Hey Fred, have you ever gone to bed with a girl?"

I was shocked. I tried not to look too embarrassed, but I could feel my cheeks change color. *Good grief,* I thought to myself, *give me a break. I'm only in seventh grade!* As I recall, I pretended to choke on a piece of popcorn to stall for time. Just then his mother walked in with a couple of Cokes, and he never brought it up again. I was safe, at least for a while.

But that night I had trouble falling asleep, and it was not because of the movie we had seen. For the first time in my life my values were challenged, and I didn't know how to handle it. Somehow I instinctively knew that night was only the beginning of feeling pressure to compromise my values and lower my standards in order to avoid the embarrassment. I felt insecure. I guess I never knew what values were before that night. I still wasn't sure, but I felt the pressure, and it frightened me.

The pressure I felt that night in junior high was nothing compared to the pressure I would feel in high school and later in college. It is the same pressure that is felt a million times every day in hallways and locker rooms of campuses across our country. Fact is, moral values are mocked. For the most part, our generation has tossed values aside. Teenage virgins are in the minority. In fact, they are on the list of endangered species. Everyone who refuses to take her clothes off and "mess around" gets laughed at. Values might be invisible, but they sure stand out when people disagree with them.

Let me ask you a question. Have you ever felt pressured by your friends to lower your standards? Have you ever done something you knew was wrong just to avoid embarrassment?

Jennifer is eighteen and lives in New York City. She said, "It was like I was the only virgin left. I felt like I had a disease. I did it just to get it over with. It's no big deal."

I feel sorry for Jennifer because sexual intercourse *is* a big deal. It is not something to be done just to gain social acceptance, like swallowing goldfish or eating raw eggs to gain entrance into a fraternity.

I know there are many Jennifers who have thrown away something very special in order to avoid the pressure from the crowd. In fact, in one way or another we are all Jennifers. We have probably all compromised convictions just to be accepted. And we have all lost something precious in the process.

These things called *values* are precious. They are intended to protect us and help us survive. It is my goal that before you finish this book, you will not only understand what values are, but you will select values on which you can build your life. Values are foundational. Until we get them firmly in place, we don't have a leg to stand on.

TIME-OUT

More than 11,000 people attended funeral services to pay tribute to Len Bias. Jesse Jackson said to the crowd, "Stop and give Len Bias a tremendous round of applause," and for almost three minutes the standing ovation thundered through the same field house where Len Bias had electrified the fans with his basketball genius. As the crowd sat in the seats from which they had watched his body twist for rebounds and vault for jump shots, they couldn't help but feel disappointed, almost as if Len had broken a promise.

When Red Auerbach stood up and talked, he admitted, "I felt closer to Lenny Bias than any kid I've ever drafted. He would have been a great star." People wept. When Maryland's coach, Lefty Driesell, retired Bias's No. 34 jersey, everyone clapped again with tears running down his cheeks.

Most people that day experienced a head-on collision of emotion. They celebrated a stunning college career and cried for an aborted professional career. They cheered for the thrilling memories and swallowed hard for what might have been. They would gladly have met there that day to cheer Bias on, retire his jersey, and honor him with applause, if he were gone because he had joined the world-champion Boston Celtics. But instead of leaving there with scores of pages yet to be filled in the life-journal of Len Bias, they each had to take Bias's journal and write, "The end." The empty pages will remain empty.

My friend, your life-journal is not full. There are many pages yet to be written. You are too young to die. Now is a good time for you to call time-out so you can thoughtfully choose a value system to live by.

For Discussion

1. Whose fault was Len Bias's death?

2. Why are values called "a matter of life and death"?

3. Which of your parent's values do you agree with? Which of your parent's values do you disagree with?
   When you disagree, how do you respond? Do you talk? Do you scream? Do you lock yourself in your room and pout?

4. Honestly answer the following value judgments from your perspective:
   ▸ Is it wrong for you to smoke marijuana?
   Yes ☐ No ☐ Sometimes ☐
   ▸ Is it wrong for you to disobey your parents?
   Yes ☐ No ☐ Sometimes ☐

- Is it wrong for you to cheat on an exam?
  Yes ☐ No ☐ Sometimes ☐
- Is it wrong for you to lie?
  Yes ☐ No ☐ Sometimes ☐
- Is it wrong for you to look at pornography?
  Yes ☐ No ☐ Sometimes ☐
- Is it wrong for you to take off your clothes in the backseat of a car with your boyfriend or girlfriend?
  Yes ☐ No ☐ Sometimes ☐
- Is it wrong for you to get an abortion?
  Yes ☐ No ☐ Sometimes ☐

5. Why do some people mock others who hold to moral standards?

6. Take out a piece of paper and write Len Bias an imaginary letter. Pretend you could turn back the clock to the night before he freebased cocaine. Give him advice as to how he should handle the pressure to give in to drugs.

2
When Poison Tastes Good

THE reason it is difficult to choose a set of values is that our generation lives in an upside-down world.

News reporters recently told about a most unusual crime. Thieves broke into a department store, and even though they tripped the burglar alarm, they slipped out before they were caught. When the manager and store owner arrived, they were pleased to find all the merchandise accounted for. Not a single item was missing.

However, the next day when a customer came to the checkout counter to buy a three-piece suit marked $5, they realized something was wrong. Another came to buy a silk dress marked $2.95. Another brought a plastic bracelet marked $450 and a pair of rubber thongs marked $275. Before long, it became apparent that the thieves who slipped in and out during the night had no intention of walking off with anything. They simply wanted to switch the price tags.

Our generation has been unaware that an enemy has sneaked into our society and switched the price tags. At first an alarm might have sounded, but

we didn't pay attention. We have been ripped off—
and we didn't even notice.

PUBLIC SCHOOL SYMPTOMS

A college president in Dallas, Dr. Watson, published a report that knocked the wind out of many
people. He went back in the annals and researched
the student crimes in public schools across our country in 1940 and then did the same for 1980. His figures
will probably knock the wind out of you too.

In 1940 the crimes listed as the worst offenses
in school included the following:
- chewing gum
- running in the hallways
- improper dress, specifically, leaving shirt-
  tails out
- talking
- failure to put paper in the wastebaskets

By 1980 the worst offenses in public school had
changed to the following:
- robbery
- assault
- theft and burglary
- arson and bombing
- carrying concealed weapons
- murder

The reason public schools are so sick is because our moral values have been polluted. Steven
Muller, president of Johns Hopkins University, left the
teeth of higher education rattling when he said, "The
failure to rally around a set of values means that universities are turning out potentially highly skilled
barbarians." Forty years earlier, President Franklin

Delano Roosevelt said, "[To] train a man in mind and not in morals is to train a menace to society."

The symptoms show our society is not only sick, it is floating belly-up! The reason is quite simple: when you switch price tags and turn your values upside down, everything else gets out of balance.

FALSE PROPHETS

A prophet is not some religious guru with a beard, prayer beads, and a holy book who sits for hours with his legs crossed in front of a crystal ball predicting the future. Every generation has prophets. A prophet is *anyone who shapes the values of their generation.* Today, our prophets come in many shapes and sizes:

▸ Rock stars who gyrate on stage and suck up the worship of fans while they preach about the pleasures of having sex, taking drugs, following Satan, and drinking blood.

▸ TV ad agencies who make their products seem indescribably delicious. (By the time the average kid is in first grade, he has watched 20,000 commercials. That's a lot of programming.)

▸ Hollywood film producers who show the beautiful side of violence, murder, adultery, marijuana, power, money, divorce, homosexuality, rebellion, cursing, jealousy, drunkenness, deceit, irreverence, manipulation, intimidation, and the rest.

We have heard them, seen them, and sometimes believed them. They are on the cutting edge of opinion-making in our generation. The clothes they wear affect the clothes we buy. Their hairstyles are copied. Their words become our mottos. Their posters hang on our walls. But the problem is, many of them preach lies. Their videos and amplifiers belch out foul-smelling words like:

▸ I'll show you where it's at . . .
 Make lots of money.
 Have lots of sex.
 Get a little cocaine floating around your brain.
▸ Don't mess around with . . .
 Jesus—He's not too cool!
 Morals—don't take yourself too seriously!
 The straight life—it's only for old ladies and wimps!

When rock stars like Boy George, Peter Townsend, Eric Clapton, and Keith Richards all admit to being heroin addicts, it sends a message to teenagers. When actresses and models like Farrah Fawcett, Cybill Shepherd, Princess Caroline, Ursula Andress, Grace Slick, and Hayley Mills all get pregnant before getting married, it has an effect. When we watch Goldie Hawn, Jane Fonda, Dolly Parton, and countless others smoke marijuana on a TV movie seen in our living rooms, it lowers our resistance.

THE SMELL OF GARBAGE

One morning I asked my garbageman how he could handle the horrible smell of everyone else's garbage. He said something very profound, "Before I took the job, I wondered the same thing. The first two weeks were disgusting; I thought I would have to quit. But ever since then I've gotten used to the smell. It doesn't bother me anymore. I guess you can get used to anything."

Wow! Maybe as a generation we have grown accustomed to the smell of garbage.

We have grown accustomed to the smell of extramarital sex—sex before and after marriage. Sex with the opposite sex. Sex with the same sex. Even when the rotten egg of 10 million cases of herpes and 30,000 cases of AIDS blows past our nostrils, we still can't recognize the rotting corpse of our society. Yet despite all the scares, in the past three years prostitution has increased by 300 percent. And since the Supreme Court legalized abortion on January 22, 1973, 20 million babies have lost their lives.

We've grown accustomed to the smell of suicide. Teenagers make suicide pacts and leave their car engines running in a closed garage or blow their brains out in history class to the tune of 400,000 attempts a year, but it doesn't strike us as peculiar. Most of us know someone who has tried to kill himself.

We have grown accustomed to the smell of crime. This year over one million teenagers will be arrested, and the FBI estimates vandalism in schools will cost $600 million, but it sort of blends in with the other odors.

We have grown accustomed to the smell of divorce. Every year two million more children are forced to live with only one parent, but that aroma has been around for a while, and so we hardly notice.

We have grown accustomed to the smell of beer, wine, and marijuana. Despite news reports that over three million teenagers have alcohol-related problems and the number of druggies is still on the rise, it's just one more flavor mixed in the brew.

As my garbageman friend said, "I guess you get used to anything."

DOWNSIDE UP

A number of years ago, scientists performed an interesting experiment. They strapped a strange set of eyeglasses, which looked like binoculars, on several people. The participants willingly wore these glasses every hour they were awake. Inside the lenses, several mirrors enabled the wearers to see everything upside down. At first they tripped over furniture and were unable even to walk. They could barely sit upright without falling over.

After a few weeks of wearing the glasses, their eyes adjusted and they were able to see everything rightside up again. They could not only sit up and walk without problem, they were able to drive through traffic and even ride a bicycle without difficulty. The human brain made adjustments, and each person was no longer aware of seeing upside down. As far as they were concerned, they were seeing rightside up.

Little did they know, however, that when the glasses were removed, the experiment had just begun. One by one, as the participants removed the glasses, they immediately fell over. Their brains had adjusted so well to seeing through the inverted glasses that when the participants removed them, everything they saw seemed to be upside down. It took several weeks for their brains to readjust to not wearing the glasses, but eventually each of the participants was able to see the world rightside up again.

For too long our generation has been seeing life through a strange set of eyeglasses. Everything has appeared rightside up when in fact, it has been upside down. We have been listening to false prophets. We have been shopping in a department store where the price tags have been switched. Our own flesh has been rotting, and we haven't even noticed the smell. We are in trouble when we reach the point where poison tastes good.

On live closed-circuit TV from Massachusetts, a seventeen-year-old boy drank cyanide-laced Kool-Aid on a Wednesday night comedy act. Moments later when he fell over, everyone thought it was a big joke. Then the laughter stopped. They ran onto the set, urged him to get up, but he never did. He couldn't. He was dead. The station manager admitted, "We've had some rather extreme things on the show . . . it fit so well into the entire speech. He said he would die . . . it was tongue-in-cheek humor. He was joking. But what he did was serious."

It was serious alright! But the condition of our generation is also serious. Too many people think that cheap sex, pot, and violence are just a big joke. They're no joke. They're like drinking poison; people are dying. It is time to wake up.

A WARNING

I saw a bumper sticker that reminded me of our generation. It read, "I'm lost, but I'm making excellent time."

The Hebrew prophet Isaiah warns the society that has upside-down values:

> Woe to those who call evil
> good and good evil,
> who put darkness for light
> and light for darkness,
> who put bitter for sweet and
> sweet for bitter (Isaiah 5:20).

"Whoa!" is what you say to a team of wild horses galloping blindly toward a cliff. You grab the reins in your hands, rear back and scream, "Whoooaaa! Whoa horsie!" *Whoa* means, "Change your direction immediately or suffer drastic consequences permanently."

Similarly, God grabs the reins of a generation galloping like runaway horses headed blindly toward a cliff and screams, "Woe! Knock it off immediately or suffer drastic consequences permanently."

For Discussion

1. Make a list of the crimes committed by kids in your school. Ask your parents or some other older person to make a similar list of crimes committed by students when they were in school. Compare the lists.

2. Define the word *prophet*.

3. Define *moral standard*.

4. Why do people have different moral standards?

5. When the seventeen-year-old kid in Massachusetts drank poison on live TV, why did people
laugh?
Why did people stop laughing?
How does this illustrate our generation?

3

The Rip-Off

VALUES are the standards we use to determine worth. Every day they help us decide where to spend our money, our thoughts, our time, and our energy. In other words, they keep us from getting *ripped off.*

Have you ever noticed the computerized scales used in grocery stores? Since most meat and vegetables are priced according to weight, it makes it very simple to slap twenty slices of bologna on the scale, punch in the price per pound, and get an instant readout listing the weight and corresponding value of the meat.

What we don't realize is that each of us carries a similar scale in our chest cavity which is invisible and far more sophisticated than the type used in grocery stores. In fact, this internal computer is more important to our health and well-being than our lungs and liver. It won't show up on an X-ray, but everyone has one, and if it is not programmed properly, it could prove fatal. This internal computer is the mechanism that constantly makes value judgments.

Imagine the problems that would occur in a

single afternoon at the local grocery store if the computerized scale was programmed incorrectly. Customers might walk out with a pound of beef for a nickel, in which case the store would get ripped off. Or the store might charge $20 for a pound of pickles, in which case the customers would get ripped off. Therefore, programming the computer is obviously important.

In a similar way, each of us must be sure that our internal, invisible computerized scale gets programmed properly. If it doesn't, we will be sure to get ripped off and taken advantage of. While a store's scale computes *financial values,* our own internal scale weighs *moral values.*

THE SCALE OF FRIENDS

Friends are great. You show me someone who doesn't like friends, and I'll show you a surfer who doesn't like waves. However, despite how great friends are, we can't rely on them to tell us what is right and wrong.

Wayne was a good kid. He had never been in trouble. He had never been to the principal's office. He got decent grades and was relatively nice looking. But somehow he became the target of his classmates' jokes, and he couldn't handle the pressure.

He was a little overweight but by no means obese. The kids called him "Chubby."

He was smart but not a straight-*A* student. His friends called him "Dictionary."

There were other names they called him that were far worse. From the moment he got on the school bus in the morning until he got off in the afternoon,

Wayne felt like he was under the gun of verbal abuse.

One day Wayne decided he had suffered enough. He vowed he would kill all his enemies, but of course they did not take him seriously. They never took Wayne seriously. No one realized he brought twenty-four bullets and his father's pistol to school in his gym bag.

The following article appeared in the paper (names changed):

> They were not exactly [Wayne Smith's] friends, but the kids put on their ties or dresses and came to the funeral anyway Wednesday.
>
> They came by the dozens to say they were sorry, sorry for taunting and teasing [Wayne] until he carried a .45 caliber automatic pistol into [Mr. Wallace's] first-period history class Monday.
>
> When the shooting ended at [Poe] Junior-Senior High School, 12-year-old [Wayne] was dead on the floor of Room 7, a bullet through his brain.
>
> And a 13-year-old classmate, [Tony Brown], was in the next room, bleeding to death in front of a horrified English class.

I wonder if things would have been different if Wayne's friends hadn't been so cruel. I'm sure many of them asked the same question as they sat through his funeral. But I also wonder if it would have helped if Wayne had looked somewhere else for his affirmation. Hey, his friends were lying to him. He was not chubby. He was not a dictionary or a jerk or a nerd or a weirdo. He was okay. But he weighed himself on the scale of his friends, and he felt worthless.

Sometimes friends will let us down. If we allow what other people say about us to determine the way we see ourselves, we will all, at times, feel like nerds. And if we let the popular values of our generation determine for us what is right and wrong, we will get ripped off.

Friends are fine, but they can't be the scale used to weigh our values. Jesus said, "If a blind man leads a blind man, both will fall into a pit" (Matthew 15:14). We can't let anyone else punch our buttons and program our morals. We need another scale.

THE SCALE OF FEELINGS

Several years ago singer Debby Boone released a song entitled "You Light Up My Life." The song sold millions and became the hit of the year. Since Debby is a professing Christian, many Christian magazines carried articles about her lifestory telling how much Jesus means to her. In the lyrics of the song, however, there is a line that stands out like a rotten potato. The song questions whether her feelings can be wrong when they feel so right.

That idea has been around a long time, and it has ruined more young lives than all the whorehouses in history. Our feelings are not the proper scale on which to judge right and wrong. There are billions of things that feel right that are actually dead wrong.

I read about a mother who go so irritated with her crying baby that she stuck a lit cigarette on the infant's tongue as punishment. That might "feel right," but it is sick.

For the same reason, it might "feel right" to

take off my clothes in the backseat of the car with my girlfriend, but that doesn't make it right. Or when I know everyone else is getting buzzed on weekends, it might "feel right" to go along with the crowd, but that doesn't make it right.

A missionary friend of mine, Elaine Battles, who is now in heaven, once said, "Any old dead fish can float downstream."

The Hebrew prophet Jeremiah wrote, "The heart is deceitful above all things and beyond cure. Who can understand it?" (Jeremiah 17:9). If we weigh things on the scale of our feelings, we will get cheated. Our feelings were never intended to teach us values. Instead, we actually need to take our values and teach them to our feelings.

THE SCALE OF FINANCE

Money motivates everyone. A report showed that in 1986 American teenagers spent $65 billion—that's $2,200 each! Half the money was their own, and half was mom and dad's.

We all know money is nice. Believe it or not, most of us spend $2,000 the week we graduate from high school. That includes prom dress or tux, tickets, dinner, concert, graduation night, souvenirs, prom, flowers, haircut, makeup, limousine, photographs, class ring, burgers, Coke, music tapes, videotapes, pizza, movie tickets, announcements, name cards, gas, cap and gown. We learn early that money makes things happen.

There is, however, one big thing money does not do. It does not motivate morals. If money were the most important thing in life, it would determine right and wrong. Anything that would save us or make us money would be good. Anything that would cost us money would be bad. But money is not the most important thing, and it cannot be the scale of right and wrong.

The reason shoplifting is so popular is because money is used as the scale for right and wrong. "Hey, it would be stupid to buy it when it's so much easier to steal it," some people would say.

The reason people argue for legalized gambling is strictly because they think it will make money. One reason young people often live together before they are married is to save money. The reason some young people sell their bodies in prostitution is to make money. Today, some people think we should kill unborn babies because it is cheaper. Many of the same people think we should kill the elderly who are no longer productive in society simply because it takes our money to keep them alive. These are all based on upside-down values.

I live near Miami. Down the street from my home a Brinks truck carrying thousands of dollars worth of coins tipped over. The driver rounded a curve in the road, the bags of money shifted, the weight changed, and the truck flipped. The guard in the back of the truck was completely buried by a few thousand pounds of coins. When they opened the door, all they could see were his legs sticking out of a pile of quarters and dimes and pennies.

The guard survived with only a broken jaw and a few broken ribs, but I couldn't help but chuckle at the picture of a guy caught in a pile of pennies. And I can't help but see the connection with so many of us who have sold ourselves short in life because we were motivated by money and not morals. Whenever we decide what is right and wrong according to what will give us the most money, our values get flipped upside down and we are caught in a pile of pennies.

A rare bottle of French wine that presumably belonged to Thomas Jefferson recently sold for $156,450—more than any other bottle of wine in history. While on display in a museum, it was discovered that the cork had imploded and possibly spoiled the beverage. (At that price I guess they were afraid to taste it and find out.)

It reminded me of what Jesus said, "Do not store up for yourselves treasures on earth. . . . but store up for yourselves treasures in heaven" (Matthew 6:19–20). If wine, gold, money, fast cars, and big houses were the most important things in life, they would last forever. But they don't, and they aren't.

I heard of a very wealthy man who was buried in California. Instead of being buried in a coffin, he requested that he be buried in a gold Cadillac with a fancy stereo system playing and a big fat cigar sticking out of his mouth. As the car was lowered into the hole in the ground, the crane operator was overheard saying, "Man, that's living!"

Victor Posner made his first million dollars when he was twenty-five years old. For several years he was considered the highest paid executive in the country, making an enormous $12 million annual salary. However, Friday, July 18, 1986, he was convicted of cheating the government out of $1.2 million in taxes. Victor Posner apparently lived according to the temporal value system that says money is the most important thing in life. But even personal wealth can't keep him from the law. Money might be nice to have, but it is not worth more than truth and integrity.

We need some other scale to show us what is right and wrong.

THE SCALE OF CIRCUMSTANCES

Sometimes we approach values with a let's-wait-and-see-what-happens attitude. We let the circumstances determine what we will do.

This is the approach the college coed takes when she arrives for freshman orientation and accepts an invitation to a sorority party. She says to herself, *Hey, you've got to grow up sometime. It can't be too bad. I'll go, check out what is happening, and then decide how much beer I'll drink. After all, if God didn't want me to go, He wouldn't have let me get the invitation, right?* Wrong.

One of the trends in public schools is an attempt to teach values clarification. Even third graders are encouraged to play "the lifeboat game" or the "Nazi concentration camp game" in an attempt to reprogram the child's values bank. This sounds good, but it isn't.

Here's how you play the lifeboat game. You select four students from the class to get in an imaginary lifeboat with limited food and water. You designate one kid a priest, one a pregnant lady, one a child, and one a scientist or medical doctor. Then you let the children determine which of the four should be the first to jump overboard, and which should be the last. After each of the four children is given a chance to defend his cause, the classmates are asked to vote and explain how their decision was made.

The problem with this approach is obvious. There is no point of absolute reference. What is right for one person is wrong for another. What is good in one situation might be bad in a different situation. Values are therefore only relative. As the saying goes, "The only absolute is that there is absolutely no absolute." Let me say emphatically, this approach is absolutely wrong.

Believe it or not, there are actually professors who teach that this is the best method to determine values. They call it *situational ethics,* and it says you must determine right and wrong according to the given situation.

I wonder if any of these professors attended Len Bias's funeral. I wonder how they explain the fact that their method of determining right and wrong did not work for Len.

No, circumstances must not be allowed to determine right and wrong. We still need another scale.

VACUUM OF VALUES

Not only has the attempt at values clarification in public schools been upside down, it has actually created a moral vacuum.

Even President Ronald Reagan said on his weekly radio show, "A value-neutral education is a contradiction of terms. The American people have always known in their bones how intimately knowledge and values are interwined. . . . If we give our children no guidance here . . . we are robbing them of their most precious inheritance." He suggested the downward spiral started because "the good Lord who has given our country so much should never have been expelled from our nation's classrooms."

International religious leader Billy Graham sees our generation "with almost no trusted source of guidance. Millions are simply making it up as they go along. They stumble into the future without a moral compass to guide them. . . . I find that youth want moral guidelines. They want to be told with authority what is right and what is wrong." Graham has a practical suggestion which could recommunicate values: "Prominently display . . . in every schoolroom in America . . . the Ten Commandments. I don't see how any Jew, Catholic, or Protestant could object to letting our young people know we believe in something."

Not a bad idea. (See Appendix B, "God's Ten Values.") It is certainly better than a vacuum. The vacuum created by modern values clarification is like a monster sucking up everything in its path. It is not only destroying morals but also devastating the family, the media, and the educational system. It could eventually destroy our generation. The only option is to somehow return to an absolute standard of right and wrong.

EXCUSES, EXCUSES

The reason we are lowering our values is that we are using the wrong standards, the wrong scales. Wrong standards have created a long list of excuses.

An *excuse* is "a lie wrapped in a reason." Check out some subtle lies which we have all heard:
- Just this once.
- Hey, everybody else is doing it.

▸ It's okay, I can handle it. I won't get carried away.

▸ Nobody will find out.

▸ But we love each other.

▸ How do I know it's wrong unless I try it?

▸ Financially we have to.

▸ Everybody's got to have a little fun.

▸ You can't take life too seriously.

▸ How can it be wrong when it feels so right?

All of these excuses and hundreds more just like them have one thing in common: they stink! They are lies that let us do anything we want without thinking about the consequences.

If we base our lives on upside-down values, and if we listen to these lies like the rest of our generation, we too will get ripped off.

A SWIMMING LESSON

When I was ten, I was a good swimmer and loved to bodysurf in the ocean. One day the waves were bigger than usual, and so I licked my chops, swam out past the breakers to the smooth water, and waited for my friend to join me. By the time he made it out, I was already tired of treading water. "Man, is it deep out here," he panted, "I think we better go in."

What are you, a wimp? I thought to myself. Just to test the depth I let my body sink to the bottom. It seemed to take about five minutes, and I still hadn't touched bottom, so I swam as fast as I could to the surface. When I got there, my friend called over to me, "Well, how deep is it?" Not wanting to scare the kid I answered, "What difference does it make, you can swim can't you?" The problem was, I was scared.

We swam in a little bit and waited for a nice wave to ride in to the beach. The longer we waited, the more I was psyched out. Here we were at least twenty-five feet over our heads with surf that looked like tidal waves coming at us.

"Let's take it," he screamed, and I agreed. The wave was huge. We paddled into place and before I realized what had happened, I was in midair looking down at curling white water from what seemed like three stories up. When I landed, I did so many somersaults under water I completely lost my equilibrium. I swam and swam and swam. It suddenly dawned on me, *I might be swimming sideways. I am running out of air. I might drown out here!*

I didn't know which way was up, or down, or sideways. All I knew was I was underwater and running out of time. I panicked. I opened my eyes, which I ordinarily do not do in salt water, but at that point, burning eyes were the least of my problems. It didn't help. It was too dark and muddy.

Finally, an idea popped into my brain: *Don't move. Exhale all your air. You'll sink. Then swim like crazy in the opposite direction.* It worked. When I broke surface, it was like I rose from the dead. Sucking air never felt so good. To this day I don't think I have ever held my breath for so long. It must have been at least thirty minutes (exaggeration intended), or so it seemed.

It was horrible to get overpowered by such a crushing force. It was horrible to feel trapped underwater. It was horrible not to know up from down.

The crazy thing was, my friend had a great ride. In fact, he bodysurfed the rest of the day and couldn't understand why I was sitting on the beach looking dizzy and green.

There are times in our lives when we realize we have gotten into trouble over our heads. It might be trouble with the law, or trouble at school, or trouble with our parents or girlfriend, or the crowd we hang around with. It might be the puddle of vomit between our feet that convinces us not to get drunk again. It might just be an empty feeling in our belly that says, "Hey, if anybody out there knows what life's all about, I wish you'd tell me." We feel trapped, overpowered. We want out, but we don't know where to turn.

LIFE WITHOUT VALUES

In the late sixties and early seventies, virtually every traditional value was challenged.

> ▸ *Marriage*. Why stay married to the same person? Why get married in the first place?
>
> ▸ *Sexual purity*. If sex in marriage is good, why not sex outside marriage? If sex with one person is good, why not sex with many people?
>
> ▸ *Truth and integrity*. Why not cheat on tests? If telling the truth will get you in trouble, what's wrong with a little white lie?
>
> ▸ *Life*. When the pressure gets too heavy, why not just check out? If you kill yourself, at least it won't hurt so bad.

When traditional moral values are questioned, no one remembers where they came from, so they are crumpled up and thrown away. When morality is removed, we have no way of determining right from wrong, up from down. Like being caught in an overpowering tidal wave, our heads are spinning, and our lungs desperately need to suck some air. But without morality, we aren't sure which way to swim.

Morality.   A lifestyle based on an absolute standard of right and wrong.

Immorality.   A lifestyle in violation of an absolute standard of right and wrong.

Amorality.   A lifestyle that insists there is no such thing as an absolute standard of right and wrong.

For Discussion

1. List four different ways people can determine right and wrong.

2. What scale do most people use to determine what is morally right and wrong?

3. What scale do you use to determine what is morally right and wrong?

4. What would you say to Wayne Smith if you saw him put a .45 caliber pistol to his head?
Deep inside, what did Wayne need?

5. What do you value more than anything else in the world?

Money, friends, family, God, or having fun? (Be honest.)

6. Have you ever played the lifeboat game or something similar?
Describe the game.
How did it make you feel?
What does the game teach us about values?

7. Define the term, *situational ethics*.

8. In your own words, define the following words and indicate how each one is different from the others:
   ▸ *Morality*
   ▸ *Immorality*
   ▸ *Amorality*

4

Safe Sex

ALL across our country there is a new fear of sex. Here are three letters I received from friends:

I started dating this guy 6 months ago. My parents told me not to because he is 5 years older than me, but my friends told me to go for it. He was handsome, wealthy, and popular. At first we had lots of fun. We went to the beach, concerts, out to dinner. Then all he wanted to do was go to his apartment. Every night he begged me to have sex with him. He made me feel like a nerd. Even my friends told me that sex was no big deal. They told me I should give him what he wanted. So I gave in. Ever since then, he treats me like trash. If that's what dating is, forget it.
　　　　　　　　—Glenda, eleventh grade,
　　　　　　　　Long Beach, California

I had sex with a girl, and I'm only 14. My older brother told me how good it was. He showed me all his *Playboy* magazines and told me I should start while I was young. My girlfriend is a really special person and she went along with it be-

cause she trusted me, but now we feel so dirty. I
hate myself for it, and I don't know what to do.
          —Toby, ninth grade, Glenellen, Illinois

I never had sex with anyone. All my friends
teased me and called me gay. They set it up. I had
never met the girl before. We went to a hotel
room and had sex. When we were done, she went
in the bathroom, took a shower, got dressed, and
left. When I walked in the bathroom, I read a
message on the mirror written in lipstick, "Welcome to the world of AIDS." I haven't seen her
since, but I am scared to death. I might not find
out if it's true for 5 years. I am afraid to ask anyone. What about getting married some day?
What about my family?
               —James, sophomore in college,
                   Rochester, New York

Twenty-five years ago, no one wrote letters like
these. There was a different fear of sex. Premarital
sex was socially unacceptable, and there was a pressure to abstain. Fifteen years ago, the trend changed
and people started wearing T-shirts that said, "Virginity is a sickness; help stamp it out," and "Sex is
free; have all you want." New pressures made young
people afraid *not* to have sex. The majority of our generation has given in to the pressures and thrown
morality out the window. We tried to live by the philosophy "If it feels good, do it," and we denied ourselves no pleasures—sex with the opposite sex; sex
with the same sex; sex before, during, and after marriage; sex with people; sex with animals; sex with the
living; and sex with the dead.

Now we are coming out of the sexual revolution, and we have plenty of scars to show for it. High school and college students all over the country are once again frightened by sex. We have learned that sex is not free, and virginity is not a sickness. Having tried sex without safeguards, we have discovered it doesn't work.

SEXUAL SLAVES

The sex-without-morals philosophy has caused horrifying personal destruction. Young women have been broken by unplanned pregnancies and further shattered by the painful choice of abortion. Young men felt like slaves to their passions and found themselves unable to resist immoral choices. Low self-esteem settled on top of our generation like a thick dark cloud.

I spoke to a group of students on the topic of sex. Sean sat down in the chair next to me and broke down. "I can't believe what has been happening to me. I thought I had everything under control, and now. . . ." he cried hard. "I hate myself. I wish I was dead. I am sick of sex. I am sick of bringing people down with me, but I can't stop. I'm afraid." We talked. We read some verses from the Bible to see what God had to say about sex and moral values. We prayed and hugged. He was encouraged.

As soon as Sean walked away, Beth sat down. "At first I thought it would be great to have sex. All my friends told me I should. Then I got pregnant. I was scared. I got an abortion. I've never told anyone, and I can't take it any more. Now I'm involved with another guy. I haven't had my period for five weeks. I don't know what to do."

We also talked for awhile. My heart was torn in half. I wept for these two kids and for thousands like them who were told the lie that sex is free. The so-called sexual revolution has destroyed too many lives to count. The Bible vividly describes the false prophets who started the revolution.

> With eyes full of adultery, they never stop sinning; they seduce the unstable; they are experts in greed—an accursed brood! These men are like springs without water and mists driven by a storm. Blackest darkness is reserved for them. For they mouth empty, boastful words, and by appealing to the lustful desires of sinful human nature, they entice people who are just escaping from those who live in error. They promise them freedom, while they themselves are slaves of depravity—for a man is a slave to whatever has mastered him (2 Peter 2:14, 17-19).

These revolutionaries, whose bad breath promised freedom, led our generation like sheep to the slaughter. As a result, many feel guilt, fear, loneliness, frustration, anger, and unfulfillment.

Even after the federal government has poured $500 million into sex education programs in public schools since 1973, the symptoms continue to get worse.

SEXUAL DISEASES

Besides the emotional scars, the sexual revolution has left a list of physical scars as well. In 1985 alone, the new cases of sexually transmitted diseases skyrocketed:

- ▶ 27,143 new cases of syphilis
- ▶ 910,895 new cases of gonorrhea
- ▶ 1,000,000 new cases of genital warts
- ▶ 1,000,000 new cases of urethritis
- ▶ 1,200,000 new cases of mucopurulent cervicitis
- ▶ 4,000,000 new cases of chlamydia

There are 5 to 10 million active cases of genital herpes and 25 to 40 million active cases of genital warts. Besides all this, there is now the fear of death by AIDS. In the United States alone, 18,285 persons have already died by AIDS. Another 31,834 have contracted the disease, and most of these will die within the next two years. Everyone who gets AIDS dies within a few years. An estimated one million people have the virus and could develop the disease at any time. No generation in history has ever experienced such an epidemic of venereal disease, and most young adults are scared.

CONDOMS, THE SAD JOKE

The answer given to the enormous moral problem our generation faces in now called "safe sex." It sounds something like this:

"AIDS is a deadly disease which is communicated during sexual contact between men with women, men with men, and women with women. Everyone who contracts the disease will die within approximately two years. Therefore we need safe sex, so men must use condoms whenever they have sexual relations."

This is a sad joke. Condoms don't guarantee safe sex because condoms themselves are not safe.

Thousands of married men have used condoms for years as their method of birth control, yet their wives have become pregnant. A condom can come off during intercourse, and even if it stays on, it is not airtight. Condoms were invented when Abraham Lincoln was president in 1865, and to suggest they are the brilliant new solution that will allow us to indulge our sexual appetites however we please is a sick lie.

One news commentator said, in effect, "Since AIDS can now be transmitted heterosexually as well as homosexually, the only way to be sure you won't get it is to remain a virgin, marry a virgin, and remain faithfully married to that same person." Isn't that a brilliant deduction? That is precisely what God has been saying for four thousand years. Maybe our generation is waking up to the fact that the one-night stands need to stop. Perhaps we will rediscover the excitement of God's plan for safe sex: to abstain until marriage and enjoy a sexual relationship exclusively within marriage.

BAD BREATH

It is time to stand up to rock groups and rock stars like Prince, Ozzy Osbourne, Twisted Sister, Frank Zappa, Alice Cooper, and Van Halen and call them liars. Bleached-blonde Madonna hit a raw nerve of emotional teenage life in her song "Papa Don't Preach" about keeping her illegitimate baby. Everyone dreams about a carefree, happily-ever-after teenage romance where lovers don't plan, they just get carried away. Such a life is only fantasy, however. The real world of carefree sex is one with disease, pain, guilt, broken relationships, and self-hatred. Perhaps it is time for someone to say, "Madonna, don't preach."

NO ESCAPE

Sixteen-year-old Judson (name changed) was scuba diving in an underground cave. He was an expert diver, having made about a hundred dives since receiving his certification.

Unfortunately, he had disregarded the No DIVING! sign posted near the caves and thought he was skilled enough to successfully navigate the treacherous underwater journey. But he got lost in the dark.

He knew he had only moments of air left in his tank. He unsheathed his diver's knife and etched his last message on his yellow metal air tank. It read, "I love you Mom, Dad, and Christian." They found his body the next night in fifty-seven feet of water.

Even though we may be well-trained and smart, we may disregard the warning signs. We may go too deep, get lost, and not find our way out. Thousands in our generation are disregarding the moral danger signs and getting sexually involved over their heads. They feel trapped and see no escape in sight.

THE VALUE OF SEX VALUES

Some are still wondering, "How could so much pain and human suffering come through sexual immorality?" The answer is obvious. When moral values are rejected, even the best things in life become polluted.

Human sexuality is one of the most precious treasures we have, and it must not be treated like some cheap toy. Sex is awesome. It is holy, sacred, and special. The sexual revolutionaries of the sixties and those who still practice the *Playboy* philosophy have a horribly low view of sex. Those with the highest view of sex are Christians.

I have discovered young people all across our country who are breaking loose from the chain of moral slavery. They are tired of all the worn-out lies and the bad jokes they have been told.

One of the best-selling albums among Latin American teenagers talks about waiting until marriage. The record features female vocalist Tatiana Palacios and male vocalist Johnny Correa, of the rock group Menudo. Their song "When We're Together" was number one in Mexico last year, selling 500,000 copies.

Johnny sings about kissing her lips and feeling a strong emotional response and then sings, "And you tell me to wait."

Tatiana responds by admitting she'd rather get physically involved but she won't because she knows it is better to wait.

In another song, "Wait," they mix their voices to sing about the hazards of premarital sex, including "children we can't afford."

One university student told her mother, "Last year virgins were laughed at. This year they are admired. Everyone wants to date a virgin. No one wants to marry someone carrying AIDS. We used to look at dating as a big game, but now everyone is much more serious about it. It is nothing to mess around with."

Virginity might be popular one year and unpopular the next year. The question is not what is currently popular. The question is what is valuable. We have learned the hard way that sex is not free. Sex is not even cheap. Human sexuality is valuable, and it must be protected by a strict moral standard that is able to say, "No thanks. I will wait until I'm married, and then I'm sure it will be wonderful."

Sex is safe as long as it is protected by a strict standard of morality.

For Discussion

1. For what different reasons are people afraid of sex?

2. If your friend got pregnant, what advice would you give her?

3. If someone says, "If it feels good, do it," what standards of morality are they using?

4. In your opinion, how do you respond to the slogan, "Virginity is a sickness."

5. Define *sexual slaves*.

6. Does the possibility of catching a venereal disease discourage sexual immorality?

7. When is sex safe?

5

The Big Rip-Off

AT the end of the 1985 pro football season, the New England Patriots flew into Miami to challenge the Dolphins for the AFC (American Football Conference) Championship with the winners going on to the Super Bowl. One of the Patriots players boasted to a sport reporter, "We're going to rip their faces off." Of course, as a Dolphin fan I was extremely insulted. When reporters asked Dan Marino what he thought of that remark, he replied, "Well, we're going to rip *their* faces off!"

Ripping faces off is what we do to the other team when they think they are better than we.

Ripping faces off is what we do to the other classmates when we think they are acting too cool.

Ripping faces off is what people with one set of values do to people with a different set of values. They stand up and start screaming, "Hey, you can't live like that." Then they grab our face, sink their fingernails into our cheeks, and yank as hard as they can. They are sure we are wearing a mask. But once the blood drips on our shirt, they usually let go and walk away shaking their heads.

DRAWING THE LINE

Knowing *where* to draw the line is never easy. But knowing *when* to draw the line is just as important. If we don't know when to draw the line, we will never be able to figure out where.

When you are in a car full of guys who are smoking marijuana, it is not the time to decide whether it is right or wrong to do drugs.

When you are alone with your boyfriend, and he starts unbuttoning your blouse, it's a little late to decide where to draw the line.

Regardless which values we choose, in an upside-down world we can be sure they will be challenged. People will poke them, squeeze them, chew them up, spit them out, and shoot them full of holes. If we don't have strong convictions, we will never survive the assault. If Len Bias had drawn the line sooner and stuck to his convictions, he would still be alive and setting records in the NBA. The Boston Celtics might even still be the world champions.

THE ASSEMBLY LINE

Last week a man was working on an assembly line in Michigan. He got too close to a computerized robot. The arm-clamps grabbed him and thrust him against the wall with such strength that they crushed his chest cavity, and he died instantly. The report stated that it was not so much a mechanical error as it was a human error. The robot did what it was programmed to do, but the man was just in the wrong place at the wrong time.

Just as violently, my mind thinks about all the

teenagers who have walked too close to the assembly line of the crowd and have been grabbed in the clamps of compromise, only to have every drop of self-worth squeezed right out of them.

Life is not an assembly line. Values cannot be forced on us, and those people without values must not be allowed to strip our values from us.

Once in a while when I walk into McDonalds and look at how everyone dresses, I think maybe we are on an assembly line: the same jeans, same sneakers, same T-shirts, same hairstyles, same music.

It's time we admit that we feel pressure to compromise and even do things we know are wrong just to avoid the embarrassment. It is also time we realize that such pressure is a real killer.

COPYCAT SUICIDE

Recently we have seen an epidemic of what the newspapers have called "copycat suicides." In one week we logged a horrifying record.

- *Wednesday:* Four teenagers (ages 16 to 19 years) found dead of carbon monoxide poisoning in New Jersey.
- *Friday:* Two teenagers (ages 17 and 19) found dead of carbon monoxide poisoning in Chicago.
- *Saturday:* Fourteen-year-old boy found dead of carbon monoxide poisoning in Chicago.
- *Tuesday:* Three teenagers (age 17) found dead of carbon monoxide poisoning in New York.

This is sad. It's sad when a young person, with a whole life to live, decides it's not worth it. It is sad when it appears that some might just be copying someone else's behavior.

What we don't realize, however, is that every time we copy someone else's behavior, we commit suicide. We kill the unique person we were originally intended to be when we pretend to be someone else. When we lower our moral standards just to avoid criticism or personal embarrassment, it is nothing short of copycat suicide.

Pressure from friends to do wrong is the biggest rip-off of all.

MARIJUANA MOCK

I can remember one time my friends tried to rip my face off.

When I was in high school, I drove into New York City with a bunch of friends. Six of us squeezed into my buddy's Nova, and we took off.

Before long the driver lit up a marijuana cigarette. He took a deep puff and passed it to the next guy, who also took a deep puff. "Not bad," he commented like an expert, and passed it to the next guy. He also took a deep puff and passed it to the backseat. Needless to say, I was starting to feel the pressure as the pattern developed.

The guy sitting next to me took the joint and looked at it for only a moment. He took a puff and passed it to me in the middle of the backseat.

You talk about pressure! I wasn't even sure how to hold the thing. I could tell it was going to be a long evening. I was stuck. Rather than faking it, I figured I might as well set the record straight right away. "I don't smoke," I admitted.

As I expected, the car erupted in laughter. The driver laughed so hard, he almost swerved off the road. "What's the matter? You afraid to catch on fire?" More laughter.

I passed the cigarette to my best friend next to me in the backseat, who was also a nonmarijuana smoker. I assumed he would decline since I had already taken all the flak. When he put the cigarette to his lips, I couldn't believe my eyes. I guess he felt the sting of the mocking I took and figured he would rather do anything to avoid that.

But I will never forget what happened next. As he took a puff, his eyes bugged out and then clamped shut so hard I thought he'd never get them apart again. He tried to swallow hard but there was no holding it back: COUGH! COUGH! COUGH!

You think they teased me; they laughed twice as bad at him. It was brutal! At least I had been honest enough to draw the line and let them know I wasn't interested. My poor friend compromised his convictions. He broke down under the pressure, and the rest of the guys showed him no mercy. All night long they kept handing him reefers, saying, "Hey, you want to try again? Ha, ha, ha!"

I learned something that night. Sure it hurts to get teased. It hurts when they stick their nails in your cheeks and try to rip off the mask. Pressure is never comfortable. But no matter what other people think, if I have a standard of values, it is better to be honest about it than to fake it, even if I become the target of a few jokes. After they try to rip our face off a few times, if no mask falls off, they will stop. In fact, they might even respect us for it. *Right is right, even if no one is doing it. Wrong is wrong, even if everyone is doing it.*

As young people, we understand that the decisions we make today will affect the rest of our lives. We need to be sure we draw the lines in the right places. We don't want to get ripped off, and we certainly don't want to get the life squeezed out of us.

For Discussion

1. Why do different values upset us?

2. Why is it too late to decide where to draw the line when your boyfriend starts unbuttoning your blouse?

3. Have you ever known anyone who killed himself? How did it make you feel when you learned about it?

4. For what different reasons do people commit suicide?

5. Have you ever wished you were dead? Why?

6

Who Punches Your Buttons?

JESUS is willing to arm wrestle any twentieth-century prophet. He said, "Enter through the narrow gate. For wide is the gate and broad is the road that leads to destruction and many enter through it. But small is the gate and narrow the road that leads to life, and only a few find it" (Matthew 7:13–14).

Jesus does not mess around when it comes to morals. He does not want us to mess around either. He doesn't want us to decide what is right and wrong according to rock star Billy Idol, or Hollywood star Eddie Murphy, or Joe Blow in homeroom. Jesus says that He alone has the right to show us which values are worth living for.

THE PROGRAMMER

Anyone who knows anything about a computer knows that the most important person involved is the programmer. If the machine is programmed properly, it will work well, but if it is not programmed properly, it will be useless.

Jesus wants us to understand that He alone

can program the computerized scale we carry around inside our chest cavity. He does not want just any old weirdo punching the buttons. He alone has the classified information, and He alone has received highest clearance. He takes that task seriously, and He fights for it jealously.

Specifically, the Bible says, "Do not conform any longer to the pattern of this world, but be transformed by the renewing of your mind. Then you will be able to test and approve what God's will is—his good, pleasing and perfect will" (Romans 12:2). In other words, "Do not any longer let your generation program your computer! Instead, begin letting Jesus reprogram your value system and you will experience for yourself how awesome it really is."

ABSOLUTES

We need to understand that in order to establish any value system, we need an absolute standard of measurement. In our country, the measurement we use for weight is pounds, for length it is feet, for time it is minutes, for money it is dollars. These are fixed standards of measurement.

Moral values also need an absolute standard for measurement. Without such a standard, every issue we face would be a jump ball. But fortunately, we do have an absolute standard to gauge what is morally right and wrong. The standard is God and His Word.

In a protected area of the Smithsonian Institution in Washington, D.C., we find what is known as "the perfect yard." It is a metal yardstick cut at exactly thirty-six inches with as perfect accuracy as is

humanly possible. In a sense, every other yardstick is compared to this one to determine near-perfect length. If every other measuring stick were destroyed, or if anyone challenged the measurement of a yard, we could go to this ruler in the Smithsonian Institution as our gauge.

In the realm of morals, God is our Perfect Yard. He does not change. He will not be destroyed. He is always dependable, and we can look to Him as our standard! In a day when everything else around us is wearing out, Jesus stands alone. "Let God be true, and every man a liar" (Romans 3:4).

TAKE IT FROM AN EX-DRUGGIE

My friend George has an exciting story. After a football game one night, he was invited to a party by an old girlfriend who assured him there would be no beer or drugs. When they arrived, he realized she lied. The place smelled like a brewery. He wanted to leave, but she had driven.

George knew about drugs and alcohol. When he was thirteen he got high three times a day. He spent his seventy-dollar paycheck on food and drugs. Even though he stuck with only marijuana and occasional LSD and cocaine, he felt like he was being cheated. While reading the Bible, he understood the words of Jesus, "The thief comes only to steal and kill and destroy; I have come that they may have life, and have it to the full" (John 10:10).

George was sick of wasting his life, so in his own room he got down on his knees and prayed, "Jesus, I turn over my life to You. If You will, come inside and scrub me clean. You can get rid of all the crud in my heart. You can make any changes You want. I've messed things up so bad, if You can do anything with it, it's all Yours."

Apparently when Jesus heard George say that, He went bananas. He changed George's life so much, George became like a rock. His values turned upside down. He drew lines for moral issues, and he didn't care what people thought. His life now belonged to Jesus, and nothing else mattered.

On that particular night, however, he found himself in a pressure cooker. "What's your problem," his old friends teased, "you too good for us?" Then they cut loose with the names, "Preacher Boy," "Mamma's boy," and "Georgie-Georgie the goody-goody."

What should he do? His friends think he has gone off the deep end, but that's because they don't know Jesus, and they don't know the inner change Jesus brought into George's life. He is getting his face ripped off, and he isn't even wearing a mask.

George could have looked for the easy way out, but he didn't. When the laughter subsided, he asked them to sit down, and he proceeded to tell them his story about what Jesus did in his life. He told how he had a new set of values and a purpose for living.

To his amazement, they not only listened, but when he was done, the editor of the school paper asked him if she could publish his story. She said, "I think it will be the most interesting article we have ever had."

He sent me a copy of the article, and it got me excited. Here is a real-life example of someone who not only experienced a revolution in his life when Jesus handed him a new set of values, but a guy who laid his reputation on the line and thereby became an example to the rest of his classmates. Bravo! I stand up and clap for you, George!

A VISION

Hey, can I share a vision with you?

I believe every high school and college campus across our country is waiting for a George. Our generation is dying to find young men and young women who will dare to base their lives on absolute moral values, which they refuse to compromise regardless of the consequences. You see, there are not too many Georges out there. Students are wondering if there are any answers to life's ultimate questions.

Beyond just that, I believe that right now Jesus is in the process of raising up such men and women to be examples for the rest of us. In fact, I will take this vision one step further. I believe He wants to recruit *you* to be such a leader.

THE CLOCK-SHOP STORY

The time has come for us to quit looking around to see what other people are doing before we take a stand for right and wrong. There is only one place we need to look, and that is to Jesus and what He has told us in the Bible.

Every morning a young man stopped at the clock-shop to look into the window in order to set his wristwatch. Finally, one day the owner asked the young man, "May I help you? Is there a clock you'd like to buy?"

"Oh no, thank you! I work down at the lumber mill, and I blow the whistle every day at noon. I want to be sure that I have the correct time, so I set my watch according to your clocks."

"That's funny," the clock-shop owner replied, "every day at noon I set my clocks according to your whistle."

This story is worth a grin, but it all too tragically describes what happens to a generation without absolute values. If I look at others to decide my morals, and if they look at me, then we're both in trouble. If no one has the correct time, then who blows the whistle? If no one knows for certain what is right and wrong, then anything goes.

THE SPELLING BEE

I hated spelling. One day in eighth grade, our grammar teacher gave us a surprise spelling test of fifty review words, and I was the only kid in the class who got fewer than twenty-five correct. It was so embarrassing!

This year in Newberry, South Carolina, the district area spelling bee contest was being held to determine who would represent their school district in the state competition. An eighth-grade girl, Yakina Glymph, was given a word to spell and she said, "c-e-m-e-t-e-r-y." She held her breath. The audience looked on attentively. The judges quietly discussed their verdict and then said, "Wrong!" She sat down disappointed. The judge gave the proper spelling as "c-e-m-e-t-*a*-r-y."

Some time later it was discovered that actually the judges were the ones who were wrong. Yakina had originally spelled the word properly. She was then allowed the opportunity to qualify for the state level spelling bee.

There are many times in life when we need to appeal to a higher authority in determining right and wrong. We need someone who can give us straight answers to our honest questions.

Fortunately, Someone does know right and wrong. Jesus knows what time it is, and someday He will return and blow the final whistle. Jesus also knows what is right and wrong. And the wonderful punch line is this—He has clearly drawn the lines and spelled out right and wrong for us in the Bible.

No one stands up next to God with a measuring rod to see how perfect He is. He is the Measuring Rod.

No one puts God on the scale to see if He is right or wrong. He is righteousness.

Everything is held up next to God. What is good is good in relation to Him. What is bad is bad in relation to Him. Since He is of absolute worth, He alone has the right to teach us our value system.

God is eternal, and His standards are universal. They apply to every individual in every culture in every generation. Only God could establish such a perfect standard, and only God could make it known to us. We do not live in a grab bag full of amoral choices. In a generation that has challenged every traditional value, we can point to the source of our values—God Himself. And when we wake up tomorrow, His standards will still be the same.

For Discussion

1. List three reasons why Jesus is able to help us establish a value system.

2. Define *moral absolutes*.

3. Do you know anyone like my friend George who has strict moral values?
How do you feel towards him or her?

4. What standard can we use to determine moral absolutes?

5. Make a list of six moral absolutes.

6. Which moral absolutes are you willing to maintain even if you are mocked by your friends?

7. Have you ever been mocked for holding to moral absolutes?
Describe the situation.
How did it make you feel?
How did you respond?

7

Ears to Hear

I FLY on approximately six airplanes a month. On one particular trip, as the flight attendants were running through their preflight instructions, I was aware that no one was paying any attention. A female voice over the loudspeaker was doing her best to make buckling our seatbelts sound interesting, and another flight attendant was standing in the aisle doing a live demonstration. They were doing their best to communicate, but everyone else was doing his own thing. No one was paying any attention, and it bothered me.

On my next flight the voice began, "Welcome to flight 517 to Chicago. Please give attention to your flight attendant as she demonstrates the use of your seatbelts. Place the . . . in case our cabin loses pressure; the oxygen masks will . . . slip them over your nose and mouth and breathe normally. In case of an emergency landing, the emergency exits are located in the forward and aft cabins. Your seat cushion can be used as a flotation device." No one was listening, and so I tried an experiment.

Since I was seated on the aisle, I leaned out,

opened my eyes wide, and gave the flight attendant my undivided attention. I smiled and grimaced in amazement at her every move. I even made comments like, "Wow!" "Isn't that incredible!" "I can hardly believe it!" When she was done, I stood up and applauded and said to the people around me, "Have you ever seen such a fine presentation?" When she walked past me, I stood up, shook her hand, and congratulated her on such a well-rehearsed presentation, "One of the best I've ever seen." The flight attendant was entertained, and everyone on the plane had a good laugh.

As I sat down I was reminded of all that God attempts to communicate to me, and yet how little I pay any attention. He speaks to me. He even demonstrates His love to me in so many tangible ways, and yet I hardly even notice.

VOICES

At this moment—right now, as you hold this book in your hands—there are all kinds of voices zooming past your ears, but you can't hear them. You don't have a receiver to pick up the AM/FM radio waves or the shortwave radio signals. They are just bouncing off you.

> ▸ If I listen to the *voice of popularity*, I will decide what is right and wrong based on what will gain me more friends.
>
> ▸ If I listen to the *voice of parents*, I will decide what is right and wrong based on what will gain me the approval of mom and dad.
>
> ▸ If I listen to the *voice of passion*, I will decide what is right and wrong based on what will satisfy my sexual appetites.

▸ If I listen to the *voice of God,* I will decide what is right and wrong based on what He says in the Bible.

Even though God's voice is in a league all by itself, at times it just bounces off our ears like lightning bounces off a rock.

In the last book of the Bible, Jesus speaks to seven different groups of people. He has a different message for each of the seven groups, although there is one sentence He repeats to each of the seven groups: "He who has an ear, let him hear what the Spirit says to the churches" (see Revelation 2, 3). Jesus is keenly interested in our hearing because He knows that the direction of our lives is determined by where we tune our receiver. The voices we listen to determine our values.

The Bible describes at least three distinct ear problems: itching ears, heavy ears, and uncircumcised ears.

1. ITCHING EARS

We have all had itching ears. After we go swimming, water squishes back and forth in the ear. A gnat or small insect flies into the ear, and we can't get it out. We rub it, stick our finger in it, Q-Tips cotton swab, ball point pen, crowbar, anything! When we have an itching ear, we stick things in the ear, not for the purpose of hearing better, but simply for the purpose of satisfying the itch.

The Bible says there is a spiritual condition we can get called *itching ears.* "For the time will come when men will not put up with sound doctrine. Instead, to suit their own desires, they will gather around them a great number of teachers to say what their *itching ears* want to hear. They will turn their ears away from the truth and turn aside to myths" (2 Timothy 4:3-4, emphasis added).

Those with this problem bounce from church to church, from spiritual guru to guru, searching for the latest spiritual fad. They stick things in their ears, not for the sake of learning, but just to satisfy the itch.

We know that we can get whatever advice we want. We can get certain advice from a friend at school, and other advice from our parents. We can go to people to hear whatever we want to hear.

The ear is a highly sensitive instrument, and we need to be careful what we stick into it. Our spiritual well-being depends on it.

2. HEAVY EARS

We have all had heavy ears. Heavy ears are ears that have heard and heard and heard and can't bear to hear any more. We have all listened to political speeches, school lectures, or even sermons when we have been bored to tears. We fidget, doodle, daydream, or even doze off. Heavy eyelids and heavy ears go hand in hand. God says, "Make the heart of this people dull, and their ears heavy" (Isaiah 6:10 NKJV).

Believe me, as a speaker, I think it's wrong to bore people with the Bible. However, it is not bad speaking that produces heavy ears. Good speaking that lands on bad ears produces heavy ears. Ears that get heavy under accumulated conviction to which we have never responded will produce heavy ears.

Wax is good for the ears, but wax buildup is

dangerous. Fluid is good for the ears, but fluid buildup is dangerous. Truth is good for the ears, but truth buildup can be devastating. Truth heard but not obeyed is a bummer.

When I was a student at a Christian college, I went to church three times on Sunday and to chapel five days a week, besides reading the Bible on my own. It sounds disgusting, but I got so much Bible I was getting sick of it. I found myself reading *Sports Illustrated* or listening to my Walkman during sermons, and no one even noticed. I found myself getting so smug during preaching, I hated it. Instead of letting God's Word sit in judgment over me, I was sitting in judgment over it. I knew I needed to do something about it, and so I decided to obey everything I heard. For every message I heard, I looked for one thing to obey. During every sermon I listened to, no matter how eloquent, I listened for God to show me something I could put into action. That simple habit actually healed my heavy ears. Instead of reading *Sports Illustrated* in chapel, I saved it for history class.

3. UNCIRCUMCISED EARS

Listen to this pathetic question: "To whom shall I speak and give warning, That they may hear? Indeed their ear is uncircumcised, And they cannot give heed" (Jeremiah 6:10 NKJV). It makes me sad to hear God begging for an audience. These people won't listen because they *can't* listen. Their ears are dead. There is no passage for the sound waves to enter such ears, so the waves just bounce off.

Hey gang, today in our country we have more

Christian literature, more Christian bookstores, more churches, more Christian colleges and universities, more TV and radio preachers, more teachers and evangelists than ever before in world history, and yet our generation is riding a skateboard to hell. I used to wonder why. Now I understand. We have many preachers but too few listeners. We have voices to speak the Word, but no ears to hear it.

Two bums were sitting on a park bench. One man asked the second, "How did you get here?"

"I didn't listen to anyone," he responded. "How about you?"

"I listened to everyone."

Listening to everyone is *itching ears*. Not listening to anyone is *heavy ears*. Both are *uncircumcised ears*—they don't hear from God.

At 11:40 P.M., April 14, 1912, the greatest ocean disaster took place—the sinking of the *Titanic*. The *Titanic* had been called "the unsinkable ship," and the world was horrified as it sank in the Atlantic Ocean.

What many people did not realize was that the captain of the vessel ignored warnings of ice floating in its path. For fifteen hours prior to the crash, warnings were given from at least six ships also traveling in the same waters. Only forty minutes prior to the crash, the *Californian* wired that they were stopped and surrounded by ice. The *Titanic* paid no attention. Despite the fact that it was entering into an ice-belt seventy-eight miles wide, the ship didn't even take the minimal precaution of reducing speed.

When God speaks, we need to listen. We need

to respond. If we continue to ignore His warnings, we will not survive.

HEALING FOR HEARING

It is encouraging to know that during Jesus' earthly ministry He healed the deaf. If He did that for physical ears, we can be sure He will do as well for spiritual ears. After all, our spiritual health depends on it. Just as we feed the body through the mouth, so we feed the soul through the ear.

Jesus said many times, "He who has an ear, let him what hear what the Spirit says to the churches" (Revelation 2:7). I never knew what that meant until one evening when I tried to call our two-year-old daughter Andrea in for dinner.

"Andrea, it is time to eat dinner now. Please come inside and wash up." She was standing five feet away from me looking right into my eyeballs, and she heard every word. In response, she jumped on her Big Wheel, pedaled as fast as she could down the sidewalk, spun out, and looked at me as if to say, "What are you going to do now, Dad?"

My tone of voice changed. "Andrea, did you hear me?" Obviously she did, and she couldn't have cared less. "I said it is time for dinner; now get in here." She proceeded to pedal down the sidewalk to our neighbor's driveway, spin out, and look at me with the same defiant expression.

This time everyone in the neighborhood could have heard me. I put emphasis on every syllable. "ANDREA JOY HARTLEY, you get back here right now!" She knew I had finally drawn the action line. She came home.

What was the problem? Was it her ears? No, she has two lovely ears that work fine. The problem was, she did not have ears to hear.

Ears to hear are ears that not only hear but obey. They are ears that come under the authority of the voice speaking.

LEARNING TO LISTEN

There was a time in my life when I attended a church where the preacher was so bad he couldn't preach his way out of a wet paper bag. Every Sunday I left church arguing with God, *What am I doing here? Surely there are better churches than this one. Good grief, this is disgusting. I'm wasting my time.*

In the middle of my grumbling, God shut my mouth with a simple question, "Who did you come to listen to?" The implication was obvious: Either I came to listen to a man, or I came to listen to God. As long as I was interested in listening to God, I shouldn't be disappointed because He *was* speaking. Unfortunately, His Word to my ears was bouncing off like lightning bounces off rocks.

The amazing conclusion to this story is that God taught me more about hearing His voice while listening to that preacher than while listening to other great preachers.

WINNERS

Someone has said, "There are three groups of people in the world: those who make things happen; those who watch things happen; and those who walk around wondering what's happening." God wants us to be in the first group who make things happen. In order for that to be true, we must be attentive, responsive listeners.

Every year in Europe the sheepdog championships are held. Each dog is released in a pen containing sheep, some with red ribbons and some without ribbons. The dog needs to separate the two sets of sheep, herd them through a series of fences, and direct them into two different pens. The dog owners are not allowed to say a word, but they are allowed to blow their dog whistles. The dogs are trained to recognize different pitches and different sounds in order to indicate right turn, left turn, faster, slower, back off, and other maneuvers.

The winning owner was interviewed. When asked about his dog, he simply responded, "The reason my dog won was because he was the best listener."

The reason listening is so important to God is because it hits right at the heart of what we are all about as followers of Jesus. Who we listen to determines who calls the shots, who is in control, who is boss.

Jesus said, "My sheep hear My voice, and I know them, and they follow Me" (John 10:27 NKJV).

HEARING AND ACCOUNTABILITY

When we hear someone tell us something, we are responsible to do something about it. When I spoke to Andrea and told her it was time to wash up for dinner, she was responsible to do something about it. Every time God speaks, He is looking for a response.

Do you remember what happened the first time He spoke? The world was made. The entire cosmos was created at the power of His word (see Genesis 1–2).

An investment firm ran ads on TV for years that showed very busy situations, and then someone would lean over, cup his hands, and whisper the words, "E. F. Hutton is my broker, and he says. . . ." Instantly, all the activity stops. Every head turns, eyes bulge, then another voice says, "When E. F. Hutton talks, people listen." The implication is obvious. If money is of great value to us, there is nothing more important than listening to the voice of those who know how to make it.

The question is this: *When God speaks, what do I do about it?*

Recently I stayed in a men's dorm at a college campus. I rose early, showered, and sat down to read. One after another throughout the dorm I could hear the students' alarms go off. There was one horrible alarm that kept sounding every ten minutes. I smiled as I realized the owner was hitting the snooze button time after time.

I thought about how often God tries to get our attention, and how often we hit the snooze button. We put Him off and decide to do something about it at a later date. An alarm clock give you six chances to get up, once every ten minutes for an hour. Then the alarm will not sound again.

When God speaks to us, we need ears to hear. If we are serious about choosing true moral values to live by, we can't put Him on hold forever.

For Discussion

1. How does God speak to us?
What does it mean to hear God's voice?

2. In your own words describe:
   ▸ *Itching ears*
   ▸ *Heavy ears*
   ▸ *Uncircumcised ears*

3. Define the word *accountability*.

4. What does the expression "ears to hear" refer to?

5. What is the difference between hearing and obeying?

8
Called to Be Aliens

WE need to hear from a true prophet, someone who dances to the beat of a different drummer. If such a person came along, he would probably get his head cut off.

Since most people walk around upside down because of their messed-up value system, somebody who comes along with their head screwed on straight will seem like an alien. When poet T. S. Eliot was questioned about his faith in Christ he said, "To a generation running away from reality, someone running toward it will seem like a deserter."

Let me introduce you to a guy who not only danced to the beat of a different drummer, but who ran around and smashed everyone else's drum sets. I will warn you now, the guy was radical.

His name was John. He was twenty-nine years old and lived by himself in the hills of Palestine. The way he dressed was outrageous. He wore a huge hunk of camel's hair the size of a bedspread. Have you ever seen the hair on a camel? It is ugly. It looks like the mange. In order to hold this bulky tunic so he wouldn't trip over it as he climbed the rugged terrain, he wore an oversized leather belt.

What he ate was outrageous—locusts and wild honey. I realize in the mountains there were no Burger Kings or Pizza Huts, but you'd think he could have done better than grasshoppers. The honey would not have been too bad, even though it was full of dead flies, ants, bee pollen, tree bark, and leaves. But the locusts . . . they are like upper-class cockroaches. John dried them in the sun, ripped the legs and wings off, and then added salt—almost like the original Doritos tortilla chip. Sick.

His physical appearance was outrageous. The guy was unshaven with long hair and dark skin. He obviously was lean and mean due to the strict diet he was on. Having lived out-of-doors, he had a weathered complexion and probably looked much older than twenty-nine.

Living alone, you'd think he would have been known as a hermit or a misfit. He had no car, no girlfriend, no home, no job, no college degree. But there was one thing he could do—preach! People came from everywhere to listen to him. They left their offices, their mansions, their apartment buildings, their lockers, their classrooms. Some people didn't even know his name; they just referred to him as the Voice, "The Voice of one crying in the wilderness." They were not hung up on *who he was*. All they cared about was *what he said*. When he spoke, nobody fell asleep. Nobody even yawned. He was like a torch, a flamethrower.

He preached 100 proof, full-strength Christianity. In fact, he had an unusual habit that put him

in a class all his own. When people responded to his preaching, he would walk into a nearby river with them, grab them by the shoulders, and dunk them under the water. This was a little ritual he performed so people would remember the decision they made to change and to live differently. Because of this, they called him the Dunker.

Fire draws a crowd. This guy was so hot that all sorts of longneckers and spectators came to watch. One day a whole bunch of religious types drove up in their black limousine chariots. They were dressed to the hilt in their namebrand tunics and clerical collars, with rolls of flab hanging out all over the place. They had college degrees and Sunday school perfect-attendance pins as long as their arms. They were the Bible scholars who could quote Scripture backwards and forwards. They could pray long flowery prayers like vertuosos. But as preachers, they were windbags. Snooze material.

They came waddling up to John like over-blown helium balloons—impressive on the outside, but inside they were nothing but gas. John took one look at them, and guess how he responded?

He could have bowed down and kissed their feet, but he didn't. He could have given them the right hand of Christian fellowship, but that was not his style. He took one look at them and screamed, "You bunch of snakes! Who warned you to flee God's wrath!?!" Nothing like popping their balloons!

John had no problem showing concern for messed-up people like druggies and alcoholics and prostitutes. But he couldn't handle hypocrites who thought they had it all together. He couldn't handle the fakers, phonies, and three-dollar bills. Essentially he had one word to say to his generation: REPENT.

Repent is a word we usually hear from some guy with bad breath on the street corner who grabs us by the shirt and stuffs a tract in our face, or from some TV preacher who has worked up a sweat screaming into a microphone and shaking his fist at the camera. To put it another way, the word usually turns us off.

However, despite all the abuse, *repent* is the one word our generation is dying to hear. It is the word that could have saved Len Bias's life. It is, in fact, the only word that makes any sense to a world that is upside down.

In a nutshell, *repent* means "change your lifestyle—turn your upside-down values rightside up." When you are cruising down the expressway in the wrong direction, you slam on the brakes, do a 180-degree turn, and proceed in the right direction. That's repentance.

We always hear the word *repent* from behind us. It often comes when we least expect it and from an unlikely source. John was certainly an unlikely source. And yes, they did cut off his head.

CHANGES

Repent comes from the Greek word *metanoeō*. *Noeō* means "to think, to use your mind, to have perspective on life, to value things." *Meta* means "after, behind." Together they mean "to change your mind, change your outlook, change your value system." As someone has said, "It is a revolutionary change of mind that brings about a revolutionary change of heart, and brings about a revolutionary change of lifestyle.

Repentance is:

▸ The sign that lets you know, "You've traveled too far down the wrong road; it's time to turn around."

▸ The fuel gauge that tells the driver, "You need to stop and refill your tank."

▸ The sword that slays the vicious dragon and declares, "You will go no further."

▸ The rain that waters the parched land and says, "You may now produce fruit."

▸ The conviction that tells me, "Hey, I really can change my lifestyle."

▸ The word that gives us a second chance.

▸ Your batting coach who shows you how to adjust your swing. You step to the plate, take his advice, and SMACK—over the fence.

▸ A gulp of air to a drowning man.

1. REPENTANCE IS A DECISION

Many people think that in order to repent, you need to break down and cry. They are wrong. Repentance does not start in the emotions; it starts in the mind and in the will.

While in college, I dated Britney during my freshman year. A couple years later, I started hearing rumors that made me sad about her getting involved with alcohol and drugs and loose morals. She accepted my invitation to dinner, which we both enjoyed. Afterward we sat on her porch, and with a heavy heart, I asked her if the rumors were true.

She looked off into the distance and nodded her head, "Yes."

Britney was raised in a Christian home. She had always been a good moral kid, but she had never really committed her life to Jesus. That night I appealed to her to do so. I pleaded with her. I did everything but get down on my knees and beg her to repent and surrender her life to Jesus.

As we sat there on the porch, she turned to me, looked right into my eyes, and said something I have thought about many times, "Oh Fred, I'll repent some day when I'm older, but I have too much life in front of me to start taking things too seriously." Then she said, "Some day when I'm married and have three kids, I will be at a Billy Graham Crusade. And when he gives the invitation to come down, I will cry my eyes out, go forward, repent, and give my life to Christ. But until then, it is no use trying."

She said those words twelve years and two suicide attempts ago. To my knowledge, she has still not repented.

We must understand that we cannot plan the scene of our own conversion. The Bible says, "Now is the time of God's favor, now is the day of salvation" (2 Corinthians 6:2). And again, "Today if you hear his voice, do not harden your hearts as you did in the rebellion" (Hebrews 3:7–8). Repentance does not start in the emotions. We don't need to have it until we are all weepy. Repentance starts in the will. It is a decision we make to turn our values rightside up.

2. REPENTANCE AFFECTS OUR LIFESTYLES

I spoke at a youth retreat last summer on the topic, "Fakers, Phonies, and Three-Dollar Bills." One young man was listening carefully. He started feeling so guilty during the talk that at the end he came up to me and asked if we could talk.

He explained that he lived in Florida. He was a leader in his church youth group, and his father was a deacon. On the outside, everything looked beautiful, but inside, he was a faker.

"At school, I am completely different," he admitted. "I do drugs, drink beer, mess around. I hate it. I can't handle it anymore. I've been living a double life."

He confessed his problems to me, and together we confessed them to Jesus.

"Now what are you going to do about it?" I asked.

"I guess I'll call home and start by telling my parents what a faker I've been." It sounded good to me.

"And then when I get home, I've got a lot of things I need to get rid of. I've got magazines and drug stuff. In fact, behind my house I've got a whole field of marijuana growing. I know that has got to go."

He knew that in order to really repent, his lifestyle would need to change radically—180 degrees. The only thing we couldn't figure out was how to get rid of the field of marijuana; we were afraid if he burned it, everyone in the town would get high!

Hey gang, it is impossible to follow Christ and follow the crowd. If we think we can be religious one day a week and then live like hell the other six days, we are wrong. The fact is, if we live like hell, we will probably go there. When God speaks, it's time to act. If we take Jesus seriously, we need to repent, and repenting will result in a changed lifestyle.

3. REPENTANCE CUTS ACROSS THE GRAIN

Make no mistake about it—initially, repentance is not a bowl full of cherries.

One Saturday night the phone rang. It was Mary from Colorado. She was depressed. "Things are not good, Fred. I feel like I will either have a mental breakdown, commit suicide, or get saved."

I was surprised to hear those words from her because I always assumed she was a Christian. I asked her a few questions:

"Have you ever prayed and asked Jesus into your life?"

"Yes."

"Do you read the Bible?"

"Sometimes."

"Do you attend church?"

"Sometimes."

"Do you believe that Jesus died on the cross for your sins?"

"Yes."

"Do you believe that He rose from the dead?"

"Yes."

She seemed to have the basics straight, but then something popped into my brain, "Have you ever repented?"

"Have I ever *what*?" she asked.

"Have you ever *repented*? Have you ever turned over the controls of your life to Jesus and allowed Him to call the shots?"

A long pause followed and then, "No . . . I was always afraid to do that."

As we talked further, it became obvious that she had never surrendered her will to Jesus. Even though she had said a prayer in her head, she had possibly never truly been born again. She had certainly never repented.

I read her a verse from the Bible, "Therefore, I urge you, brothers, in view of God's mercy, to offer your bodies as living sacrifices, holy and pleasing to God" (Romans 12:1). We prayed. She renounced her sin of rebellion against God's control and turned over her life to Jesus. It was excellent!

Without my knowing it, she got on a plane, flew from Denver to Miami, and drove to our church to attend the evening service. She stood and told the people what had happened in her life the night before. From there we went to a swimming pool where Mary was baptized. When she came up out of the water, everyone went bananas.

A few months later I flew into Denver and saw Mary. "How did you feel flying to Miami, coming to our church to get baptized, and publicly declaring your repentance?" I asked.

"I was miserable. I fought it the whole way. Everything in my body was saying, *No, don't go through with this.* If there was any way I could have turned the plane around, I probably would have. When you asked me to come up in front of the church and share what had happened, that was the worst. Suddenly, there was no way out of it. Deep down I really wanted to turn everything over to Jesus, but there were so many emotions fighting against it. But once I confessed it with my mouth and got baptized, I felt better about it. My emotions eventually followed along with my decision."

I saw something more clearly than ever before

through Mary's example. Repentance is first a decision. It starts in the mind, and the will and then the emotions will catch up.

4. REPENTANCE IS COMING HOME

I am glad God takes me seriously. I'm glad when He looks at me, He smiles and calls me, "Son." I'm glad He stretches out His arms to me when I've been gone for awhile and says, "Welcome home."

You know what repentance is like? Sometimes it seems sort of vague or abstract. But plain and simple, repentance is just *coming home*.

When I've been gone for a day and have been working hard, I love to come home. Sometimes I am gone for a week on a business trip. Then coming home is even more special. Some people are gone for months on a wayward binge or just for a prolonged trip. At times like that, coming home is the greatest thing in the world, especially when you know you'll be welcomed home with loving arms and a warm heart. That's the way Jesus is.

Repentance is not something we go through once a year, as if it is something to dread. The closer we walk with Jesus, the easier repentance comes. It is something that can come every day or at least every week as we direct our thoughts and lives back to Him; as we place ourselves, our time, our talents at His service. Whenever we repent, He pours out His love on us and says, "Welcome home."

Even those of us who have never known a happy home can still understand the way home ought to be. We can almost see the positive picture through our own negative experience. In fact, I've found those with broken homes have a greater appreciation for the love and parenting of God our heavenly Father. In fact, the Bible promises, "He is a father of the fatherless, a defender of widows" (Psalm 68:5 NKJV). When we decide to come home, His love touches us deeply.

The longer we are Christians, the harder it is to change. And yet, the longer we are Christians, the more we need to change. Regardless of where we are, it is good for us to consider this list and check the areas in which we need to repent:

☐ Looking religious on the outside without a relationship with Jesus.

☐ Going through all the right motions as a Christian for all the wrong motives.

☐ Expecting God's gifts without showing Him any gratitude.

☐ Faking repentance.

☐ Running my own life.

☐ Doing things to please my friends even when I know my actions displease Christ.

☐ Turning a deaf ear to Jesus, especially when He is talking about something I don't want to hear.

☐ Doing things that are just a little bit sinful so my friends at school don't think I am too weird.

☐ Doing things behind my parents' backs I'd never want them to find out about.

☐ Hiding things in my closets that Jesus would haul off to the dump.

☐ Living a double life.

YOUR CHOICE

Right now, I ask you, *will you repent?* Will you turn over your life to Jesus? Will you let Him change your value system? Will you let Him call the shots from now on? The choice is yours.

One of the greatest things about Jesus is that He does not grab our lives away from us and force us to be religious. In fact, He never wanted to start a religion. He just wants to start a relationship—with me and with you.

Not long ago in Miami, a six-year-old boy was playing with his daddy's loaded rifle. The father saw it and grabbed the gun from the kid. Somehow in the process, the gun fired and put a bullet through the boy's brain. He died instantly.

We need to understand that Jesus is not like that. He will not come and grab our life away from us. Even though He knows it would be safer in His custody, He will not force it out of our hands. Instead, He appeals to us lovingly to turn it over to Him.

Don't fake it! Don't pretend to follow Jesus if you are not ready. But if you are ready to make the decision, go for it! Use this prayer as a model to put yourself under the authority of Jesus:

Jesus, I know you love me. In spite of all the stuff I've done wrong, I know You accept me just the way I am. You hung on a cross and proved Your love for me.

Right now I open my heart. Will you come inside and scrub me clean? Take out the garbage. I admit I have not been living for You. In fact, I have been living in rebellion against You.

I let go of the controls; will You take over? I know You are risen from the dead, and I know You are more powerful than any other force. As You move inside my body, drive out my evil desires and give me brand-new desires to do what is right.

I'm excited to be Your child. It is wonderful to know that You will never leave me alone. You are with me always—twenty-four-hours-a-day for the rest of my life and into eternity. Wow!

I need direction. I need You to teach me Your values, to show me right and wrong. I am willing to repent thoroughly of everything You show me, but I definitely need Your strength.

I am well aware that my old friends will not understand the change right away, but that is okay. I will be loyal to You first. I am Your servant, and You are my Friend—even if You're the only Friend I end up with. But help me to love my old friends no matter how they respond to me. Help me to love them the same way You do. In fact, Jesus, help me introduce them to You.

My main desire is to please You. I want to make You happy because I love You. Amen.

For Discussion

1. How did you feel towards twenty-nine-year-old John who lived in the hills of Palestine? Did you like him?

What seemed odd about him?
How would people react to him today?
What was admirable about John?
What was disturbing about him?

2. In your own words, define *repentance*.
   Do you like the word?
   How does it make you feel? (angry? fearful? put-down? frustrated? neutral? excited?)

3. Who decides when it's time to repent? (you? your parents? your minister? God?)
   Who decides whether or not we will repent? (you? your parents? your minister? God?)

4. Why is repentance like "coming home"?

5. Go back to the section entitled "Your Turn" and check off any items for which you need to repent.

9

Shut the Doors

ON Sunday, March 8, 1987, a ferryboat left dock in Belgium heading towards England. Everything seemed normal. The seas were smooth, and the 400-foot-long *Free Enterprise* was cruising along without difficulty.

What no one realized was that the loading door was left slightly open, and water was filling the hull. When the captain turned the vessel, the interior water sloshed to one side and, within sixty seconds the enormous craft was belly-up. People were screaming, slamming into walls, and getting crushed under cargo. The twenty-eight-year-old assistant boatswain, whose responsibility it was to secure the doors, screamed, "It's my fault, it's my fault, I didn't lock them properly." Even the engineers were amazed that a 7,951-ton boat could flip over in one minute just because some water came in through a door left unlatched.

You and I are like boats. We cruise through life just fine as long as our doors are tightly shut. But when we open them too far and allow the world's influence inside, we can easily tip over.

My heart hurts for the assistant crewman who apparently neglected his duty and has been suffering because of it. My heart hurts worse for all the other young men and women who have not shut the doors of their hearts against the flood of filth and toxic wastes floating around in our society.

No matter how rough and tough we think we are, if we open ourselves up to the forces of evil around us, any of us could flip belly-up in an instant.

MY FRIEND PETER

My friend Peter was no wimp. In fact, he was a 220-pound bruiser. He thought he was tough. He thought he could handle anything. But despite his size, he went to pieces when he showed up at camp for the summer.

Peter had plenty of friends. At 6'6", he was the tallest kid in his high school and the star on the basketball team. His father was a professor at the local seminary, so Peter's Bible knowledge was superior. He was like a walking Bible dictionary. When he filled out the counselor's application form for the camp, he knew all the answers and sounded like a spiritual giant. There was just one problem: while he sounded good on paper, he was living a double life.

On Sunday he spouted Bible verses like Mount Saint Helens. He could pray for five minutes without coming up for air. He greeted the elderly women with a smile, a handshake, and a kiss on the cheek. He sang in the youth choir and played a mean trombone.

Then on Monday, it was like he took off the costume, flicked a switch, and let it all hang out. Mari-

juana at lunch break, four-letter words in physical education class, cheat-sheets in Spanish class, and skinny-dipping with girls after school were all part of his weekly routine.

When he showed up at camp, he expected to have the time of his life. In his duffle bag, along with his Bible and prayer journal, were his reefer papers, a fifth of bourbon, and a handful of nude pictures he clipped from his friend's magazines. He had been able to pull out the right stuff at the right time all year at school, and he expected to have the same skill at summer camp.

After only two weeks, he couldn't take anymore. When the campfire service was over, he came up to me blubbering like a baby. I couldn't believe my eyes. I had never before seen such a hunk of tiger reduced to such a purring kitten.

"Can we ... *(sob, sob)* ... talk ... *(sob, sob)* ... ?" he begged. I gently smiled to let him know it was okay to cry and motioned for him to slip away from the other campers so we could talk privately.

He opened up many things, most of which he had never before told anyone. It was late, and he was emotionally worked up, but he said things I will never forget. "I hate myself . . . I hate the double life I've been living. I wish I were dead. I can't take anymore . . . life is cruel . . . I'm a mess . . . O God, I can't stand it! Nobody knows what I've been going through . . . Nobody really knows me . . . nobody understands . . . Help me! Somebody, help me!" Many tears followed.

That night we talked briefly. We prayed. He walked quietly back to his cabin. But the next day I was hoping he would still want to talk. When he knocked on my door right after breakfast, I went bananas inside.

"Can we talk about how I can get my life straightened out?" he asked. I welcomed him, and for three hours we talked about values.

We talked about the importance of being honest—about not faking it. We talked about repentance and turning the controls over to Jesus. We talked about the pressure to compromise our convictions just to fit in with friends at school.

After we finished talking to each other, we talked to Jesus about it all. Peter prayed a wonderful prayer of commitment—one of the finest prayers I have ever heard. If I had recorded it on cassette, I would play it for you right now. He didn't leave anything out, or so it seemed.

That fall, however, when he showed up for college as a freshman, Peter lived like hell. Judging by his lifestyle, you would have thought he had dedicated his life to the devil rather than to Jesus. He lived one of the wildest, rowdiest lives in the history of his university. Many people scratched their heads in amazement.

You are probably wondering what happened. You might even wonder why I told you his story. Well, his story is really not so unusual. Many of us who make decisions never follow through or do anything about it. At times we get convicted of wrongdoing and our guilty consciences make us feel lousy, and so we say a quick prayer just to get rid of the guilt feelings. At times when we feel totally overwhelmed—like we're floating belly-up—we go through the motions of repentance in order to feel better about ourselves, without ever truly being interested in what's in it for Jesus.

Poor Peter knew the form of religion, but apparently he never experienced the power or the reality of a living relationship with Jesus. He was so close and yet so far away.

EVEN DR. K.

Just look at Dwight Gooden, ace pitcher for the New York Mets who earned the nickname Dr. K. by striking out 268 batters in 276 innings. This past year when he was accused of drunken driving and assaulting a police officer, nobody could believe it. Even teammate Gary Carter said that it didn't sound at all like the Dwight Gooden he knew. He was not that kind of person. Then when Dwight's drug test proved positive, people started putting the pieces together.

▸ 1984—Chosen National League "Rookie of the Year."
▸ 1985—At twenty years old became the youngest Cy Young Award winner with a 24-4 record and 1.53 earned run average.
▸ April 4, 1986—Missed exhibition game due to "minor accident." No such accident was reported.
▸ April 15, 1986—Had dispute with rental car agent.
▸ October 28, 1986—Skipped World Series ticker-tape parade. Mets said he "overslept."
▸ November 11, 1986—New York papers revealed Gooden has child by a woman other than his fiancee.

- ▶ December 13, 1986—Arrested with four friends in Tampa regarding traffic violation. Gooden fought and was charged with two felonies.
- ▶ February 19, 1987—Placed on probation after pleading no contest.
- ▶ April 1, 1987—Entered drug treatment center for rehabilitation. Left spring training with a 1-2 record and a 7.31 earned run average.

Hopefully, Dr. K. will close the door to all the pollution floating around him. His life could either end up in a wooden box like Len Bias, or if he makes the right choices, he has only begun to break records. Even though he is a great pitcher, his potential doesn't mean a thing unless he is protected by a consistent value system. His spectacular career, which went up like a rocket, might come down like a rock.

Dwight Gooden said recently during an interview, "In a way, I'm glad I got caught. I might have ended up like Len Bias." He admitted that he began using cocaine as a senior in high school. Now that he has been released from the drug treatment center, he has resolved, "I regret doing what I did, and now I'm trying to put something good into baseball."

ACCOUNTABILITY

I wish at this moment I could put my hand on your shoulder, look at you right in the eyeballs, and say:

God is watching and weighing every one of your actions, words, thoughts, and attitudes. Someday you and I and every single other person who has ever lived will stand before Jesus and give an account.

Considered to be one of the most brilliant men who ever lived, Daniel Webster was once asked what was the greatest thought he had ever had.

He replied, "I have thought about many things. But the most awesome, the most terrifying thought I have ever had is my personal accountability to God."

Everyone already dead will be there. All the great names that fill the *Encyclopaedia Britannica* will be there: the political leaders—Caesar and Charlemagne, Lenin and Stalin; the philosophers—Plato, Socrates, Hume, Kant, and Marx; the psychologists—Freud, Jung, and Fletcher.

This time when Jesus comes back, He will not come humbly as a baby in a manger or a young man on a donkey. He will come with all power and authority. He will pull the plug on the band. He will come to judge the earth with a sickle in His hand, and the party will be over.

"Look, he is coming with the clouds, and every eye will see Him, even those who pierced him; and all the peoples of the earth will mourn because of him" (Revelation 1:7).

The fact is, you and I will be exposed.

CONFESSION

There are two reactions to our accountability to God. First, we shudder, "Oh no! God is the Judge and He knows everything about me." That's frightening.

Have you ever been standing on the edge of a cliff, perhaps the Grand Canyon? Or have you ever looked out the window of a very tall building? You say to yourself, "Wouldn't it be horrible to fall from up here?" Meanwhile, a friend (or at least someone you thought was your friend) sneaks up behind you and gives you a nudge. You have a huge adrenaline surge. Your heart thuds. Your life passes before you. Every bodily mechanism prepares for free-fall. You think it's all over, but you come to your senses and realize he was holding on to your belt-loop. That is somewhat similar to considering standing before God Almighty to give an account.

Our second reaction to our accountability to God is, "Yes, God is the Judge and yes, He does know everything about me, so I might as well come out of hiding."

Sometimes we live like the band will play forever, like the music will never stop, like the beer won't run out. We think we will dance the night away. The rock group AC/DC sings a song, "Highway to Hell," that describes hell as a big party where all our friends will be.

Some think they will run up to Jesus when they die and say, "Hey, slap me five; I'm glad I'm alive." Others think they will run up and give Him a big hug and tell Him how grateful we are.

I've got news for you. Every tongue will be stopped. Every mouth will hang open, unable to even stutter. It will be instant paralysis.

John the apostle knew Jesus perhaps better than any man. They fished together, cooked together, camped together, prayed together, wept together, and laughed together. John rested his head on Jesus' chest and heard the divine heart beat. But when John saw Jesus after He had ascended into heaven, John fell at Christ's feet as though dead (See Revelation 1:17). Now, if John, who knew Him so intimately, responded like that, how will we respond when we see Jesus in all His power and glory?

The Bible says, "We shall all stand before the judgment seat of Christ" (Romans 14:10 NKJV). "Nothing in all creation is hidden from God's sight. Everything is uncovered and laid bare before the eyes of Him to whom we must give account" (Hebrews 4:13). That's awesome!

Everyone currently living will be there: all the jocks—Jabbar and Dr. J., Marino and Montana, Hagler and Leonard, Strawberry and Gooden; all the Hollywood stars—Michael J. Fox and Jane Fonda; all the rock stars—Bowie and Jagger and Jackson; all the nationalities—Chinese, French, Hispanic, African, and Anglo. We will all be there.

Coming out from hiding is exactly what God wants from us. He has been seeking our friendship ever since Adam and Eve ran and hid themselves. Rather than saying, "I can't hide anymore," we can now say, "I don't need to hide anymore."

Hey, if we have been faking it, remember this: We can fool some of the people all the time, and we can fool all the people some of the time, but we can't fool all the people all the time, and we can't fool God any of the time.

If we have left a door open to the evil force at work in our generation, God loves us too much to let us get away with it for long. We need to shut the door, or before long we will be floating belly-up. It's our choice. Why not come out from hiding and tell Jesus right where we're at? It does no good to hide. He sees everything anyway.

For Discussion

1. What does the capsized ferryboat teach us about moral standards?
   How would you feel if you were the assistant crewman who was responsible for shutting the cargo door?

2. Have you ever know anyone like my friend Peter who seemed very religious on the outside but lived a double life?
   How did you feel towards this person?

3. Define *hypocrisy*.
   Describe a *hypocrite*.
   How do you feel towards hypocrites?
   How do most people feel toward hypocrites?

4. Have you broken a commitment with God?
   Describe the specific commitment and then describe the failures.
   How did it make you feel about yourself?
   How did it make you feel about God?
   What effect did it have in your life?

5. What does Dwight Gooden teach us about moral values?

6. In your own words, describe the *judgment day*. Who will be judged by God? Do you think you will be judged by Him?

7. What is "the fear of God?" Are we supposed to fear God?

8. What will it be like to stand before God? Describe how you will feel at that time.

9. What does the author mean by "come out from hiding"?

10
What Is in Your Closet?

ON the front page of the paper was the headline, "Land Mine Backfires, Kills Teens." The picture showed a home that appeared to have been hit by a bomb. In a sense it was.

The article told about the two Miami teenagers who loved to play war games, often dressing in army fatigues. Somehow they got their hands on a land mine that contained more than a pound of C-4 plastic explosives. The mother of one of the boys had even seen the mine in a green canvas case. It was small—only 10"x6"—and heavy. She assumed it was part of their ROTC program, and since it didn't match the room decor, she moved it behind the dresser.

A few days later, the boys were handling the mine, and it exploded. It blew off the roof and destroyed two of the walls. One of the boys was blasted right out of the house, minus an arm and half a leg. He died an hour later at a local hospital. He was sixteen. The other boy died instantly and was buried in the rubble. He was fourteen.

The question I want to ask you is: *What's in*

your closet? Behind your dresser? In your drawers? What are you hiding?

Okay, probably none of us have a land mine. But we might have something just as explosive and just as life-threatening. If we have anything that contradicts the absolute moral standards that God has communicated, we might be in danger. If we have anything that irritates our conscience, something we would be embarrassed for our mother to discover, we might be worse off than we realize.

A STORY: "THE UNEXPECTED HOUSEGUEST"

I want you to imagine this scene. It is dark outside. You are home all alone—the only one in the house. The doors are locked. You are in your room. You hear footsteps coming down the hallway. You freak out! You breathe shallow, hoping this intruder will not realize you are in the house. Your thoughts race wild. *Should I jump out the window? Crawl under the bed? Grab a baseball bat to fight him off?* But you are frozen with fear. Petrified.

Before you have a chance to do anything, there standing in the doorway looking right into your eyes is Jesus. *Far out!* You breathe a sigh of relief even though you're not sure what is happening. You have prayed before, read Bible stories, and you know He rose from the dead, but you sure never expected a personal visit—not in flesh and blood anyway.

"Nice room," He says with a smile as He walks right in and sits on the corner of your mattress.

You don't know quite what to say, and so you just take a big gulp to be ready in case He asks you a question. Just by the way He looks you right in the

eyes, you know He loves you, but you still feel on edge. You wish He would have given you a little warning. After all, the room is a mess. There is crud all over the place.

"Do you have a Bible?" He asks.

You grab one off your nightstand, which was certainly sitting in the right place. You hope He is impressed.

He opens it and starts reading, "Jesus entered the temple area and drove out all who were buying and selling there." It sounds weird to have Jesus read something to you from the Bible, especially something He was personally involved in. "He overturned the tables of the money changers and the benches of those selling doves. 'It is written,' he said to them, 'My house will be called a house of prayer, but you are making it a den of robbers'" (Matthew 21:12–13).

Then He closes the Bible, looks at you with caring eyes that convince you He already knows everything about you. It is as if He sees right through you. You feel exposed, and yet you feel accepted. Everything is cool. Then, without moving from the corner of your bed, He begins looking around your room. You know He not only sees the stuff hanging from your walls, He sees what's in the drawers and closet. His X-ray vision sees what records and tapes you own.

Once again He looks you in the eye and says, "Today, I have come to your house for spring cleaning. I love you. You are my child, and I want to help you haul off to the dump some of the garbage that only interferes with your life."

At first you think He is talking about the dirty socks, gum-wrappers, and old homework papers all over the floor. At once you realize He is talking about those immoral things you have been hiding. You hang your head. Your face turns red. You wish things were different but realize you can't get out of it. You force yourself to look toward His spot on the mattress, but He is gone. He vanished as quickly as He came.

You are alone again in your room, and yet everything is different. Jesus is not there physically, yet you are more aware than ever that He is spiritually very much present with you. You have a new desire to clean house, to remove everything that is hazardous to your moral values.

You start talking to Him aloud, "Wow, Jesus, that was wild! I can't believe it! I mean, I guess I *can* believe it. You can do anything. But now I know You really care about me. You actually care what happens to me. You have my best interest in mind. Sure, I'll clean house. You show me where to start. Whatever You want me to trash, consider it gone!"

THE STORY EXPLAINED

Imagining that scene is not unrealistic. Just because Jesus is not physically present doesn't mean He is absent. Just as He took a bullwhip in His hands to cleanse the temple in Jerusalem, so He desires to cleanse our homes as well. We need to give Him the freedom to shine the light of His Word into our homes and point out what needs to go.

When we do spring cleaning, we are never

quite sure what we might find in the closet. We always discover things we had forgotten about, or things we had grown accustomed to.

If we take seriously the fact that Jesus lives with us all the time, and that our homes and lives and bodies belong to Him, it is not unusual for Him to require a thorough housecleaning. He might ask us to knock out a few walls and renovate things. After all, He has authority. And not only that, He also knows what's best for us. He knows which things fascinate us, and He also knows how dangerously explosive some of them might be.

FOUR SEARCHLIGHTS

We need to give Jesus the freedom to take the searchlight of God's Word and shine it in our closets and cupboards.

There is one verse in the last book of the Bible that exposes four big areas of darkness that will cast an evil spell on the final generation. We need to be sure we are not under their curse. Check it out: "Nor did they repent of their murders, their magic arts, their sexual immorality, or their thefts" (Revelation 9:21). Let's consider each of these four areas carefully.

1. MURDERS

God says murder pollutes the land (see Psalm 106:38), yet television is full of murder. By the time we graduate from high school, we have watched an average of 18,000 murders on TV. For some reason, the United States is big on murder. Last year there were more cold-blooded murders in St. Louis than in all England and Wales, and more murders were committed in Miami than in France, Germany, Italy, and the British Isles combined.

Rock music is becoming more and more preoccupied with murder. Rock videos drip with violence. Ozzy Osbourne's song "Suicide Solution" has been accused of promoting teen suicides. Alice Cooper produced an album entitled *Killer*. He sings "I Love the Dead" and "Hallowed Be My Name."

Billy Idol seems to be preoccupied with death, singing songs entitled "Fatal Charm," "The Dead Next Door," and "Dead on Arrival." Twisted Sister sings songs entitled, "Destroyer," "Under the Blade," "The Beast," and "Burn in Hell." The Blue Oyster Cult sing a defiant song, "(Don't Fear) the Reaper."

Heavy metal rock band AC/DC's song "Highway to Hell" suggests that death and hell will be a great party time where all our friends will be present. Another AC/DC song, "Night Prowler," says, "You lie there naked like a body in a tomb." The album jacket of *If You Want Blood* has a picture of a guy stabbed through the belly with a guitar with bloodstains all over his white shirt. Songs on this album include "Hell Ain't a Bad Place to Be" and "Rock n' Roll Damnation."

The group Metallica sings "Whiplash," encouraging listeners to bang their heads against the stage until they bleed. The song lyrics claim, "We are gathered here to maim and kill."

This spell of violence, death, and suicide can even be linked to children's toys like Garbage Pail Kid Cards that show bleeding babies speared through the chest with safety pins. Even Christian Dior manufactures a perfume called "Poison."

All such garbage needs to go. We need to obey Jesus and haul it off to the dump.

2. MAGIC ARTS

This word does not refer to tricks like pulling rabbits out of hats or sawing people in half. This refers to two specific areas: occult activity and drugs.

God has put a special curse on all sorcery, witchcraft, fortune-telling, white magic, black magic, astrology, seances, Ouija boards, satanism, and tarot cards. Several years ago, however, when the occult hit Hollywood with movies like *The Exorcist, Poltergeist, Friday the 13th,* and others, it was like the paper hit the fan. More and more young people became more than just curious about the demonic.

More teenagers read their daily horoscopes than any other age group. One occult mail-order company has a mailing list of over four million, and they get orders from a half-million people every year with an average purchase of ten dollars.

Rock music has been injected with a lethal dose of satanic stuff. Iron Maiden's album *Iron of the Beast* suggests they control the devil through their music. Black Sabbath is reported to give altar calls at the end of their concerts for young people to give their lives to Satan. On their album *We Sold Our Soul for Rock and Roll,* they sing songs entitled "Voodoo," "Die Young," and "Children of the Grave."

The rock group Venom produced an album entitled *Welcome to Hell.* The song titles include "Sons of

Satan," "Welcome to Hell," "Schizo," "Poison," "Live Like an Angel (Die Like a Devil)," "1000 Days in Sodom," and "In League with Satan." On the back of the album jacket they state, "The death of you, God/ we demand."

The term *magic arts* comes from the original word, *pharmakia,* from which we also get the word *pharmacy.* It also refers to the use of drugs. Witches were the original potheads and opium freaks. They would get high in order to make it easier to contact demons. Pathetically, today millions of young people are getting in bondage to Satan through the use of drugs without even knowing it.

We need to dispose of all drugs, drug paraphernalia, demonic materials, and music with drug-related lyrics. They are all cursed by God and forbidden to His followers.

3. SEXUAL IMMORALITY

The word from which we translate "sexual immorality" is *pornea.* You can probably recognize in it the roots of the English word *pornography.* This refers not only to sexual intercourse outside of marriage, but also to other sexually arousing habits that are plainly forbidden in the Bible.

Porno pictures are as easy to collect as baseball trading cards. You can get a front view, side view, back view, top view, or bottom view. Our TVs now carry movies into our living room that we would have been embarrassed to watch a few years ago in the theater. Even many billboards, bumper stickers, posters, and album jackets reveal things that should be kept private.

Pornography includes not only magazines, but also music. What started subtly in rock music is now explicit. Madonna sings "Like a Virgin." Van Halen sings "Hot for Teacher." Cyndi Lauper sings "She Bop," apparently about masturbation. Prince in concert jumps from one sexual gyration to another, and his fans gaze at him with their tongues hanging out, loving it. Dee Snider, the songwriter for Twisted Sister who calls himself "a Christian," admits the title of their fan club SMF stands for "Sick Mother—, Friends of Twisted Sister." Alice Cooper's "Billion Dollar Babies" talks about masturbating with a rubber doll.

Hey, if we don't wake up and not only shut the doors tight but run the bilge pump day and night, we will go down with the ship. Our generation is experiencing a flood of filth like never before. Jesus predicted, "Because of the increase in wickedness, the love of most will grow cold" (Matthew 24:12). We are living in the days Jesus talked about. Our generation may be the final generation.

Porno pictures, videocassettes, magazines, music, even the repertoire of dirty jokes need to get hauled off to the nearest dumpster.

4. THIEVERY

Believe it or not, when I was growing up I had only one friend who stole things from a store. At least, he was the only one who bragged about it. Today shoplifting is big business. Over a a million teenagers are charged with shoplifting every year, and that does not include those who never get caught.

It is happening all over the world. Two men

caught in Seoul, Korea, had been stealing bikes for the past ten years. Authorities estimated those two men alone stole 40,000 bikes valued at close to $2 million.

Nine teenagers in Salem, Massachusetts, ran through their high school breaking 200 windows, tossing computer terminals from the third floor "just to watch them smash," and vandalizing everything in sight. Yes, they were drunk, but in less than an hour they had destroyed $750,000 worth of supplies. The FBI reports that school vandalism costs $600 million every year.

Almost thirty years ago, President Dwight D. Eisenhower prophetically stated, "Today we seem to be plunging into an era of lawlessness, which in the end can lead only to anarchy. The anarchy is a destroyer of nations . . . there is something seriously wrong with our public and private attitudes towards law and order. Perhaps the basic problem is apathy, plus neglect of certain fundamental moral principles."

Let me ask you a personal question: Do you have anything in your closet or in the drawer that you ripped off? Think hard. If so, guess what you need to do with it? You need to swallow hard, tell Jesus you were wrong in stealing it, and then take it back to the place you found it. If necessary, offer to repay any damage. If you're not willing to do that, don't kid yourself by thinking you are coming clean.

DUMPSTERS, ANYONE?

We need to let Jesus cleanse our homes by removing all physical objects that are objectionable. We need to haul them to the dump.

▸ *Things we look at*—No more raunchy TV, videos, MTV, HBO, cable, or soap operas, which stink from the odor of adultery. No more pornography—all the magazines and clippings get burned!

▸ *Things we listen to*—Radio stations, cassettes, albums. All sick secular rock music and all sick secular country music get trashed.

▸ *Things we taste*—Alcohol, nicotine, junk food, marijuana, cocaine, and the rest. The Bible says, "Wine is a mocker and beer a brawler" (Proverbs 20:1). That means Bartles and Jaymes Premium Wine Cooler is a mocker. Budweiser is a brawler. They all need to go!

▸ *Things we do*—All white magic, black magic, astrology, fortune-telling devices, Ouija boards, Dungeons and Dragons and Masters of the Universe games, drugs. They are all forbidden. God says, "Come out of her, my people, so that you will not share in her sins, so that you will not receive any of her plagues" (Revelation 18:4).

The Old Testament teaches that certain objects are "devoted to destruction." They are under God's curse, and His curse is on those who mess with them.

One group of Christians in the early church took this message seriously and repented dramatically. Read what the Bible says of them: "A number who had practiced sorcery brought their scrolls together and burned them publicly. When they calculated the value of the scrolls, the total came to fifty thousand dracmas" (Acts 19:19). A dracma was a day's wage. If you figure the average laborer today earns $50 a day, then their value was equivalent to $2.5 million. That is what I call housecleaning!

Jesus is not physically in your room with you, but He is there in Spirit. Will you ask Him what you need to get rid of?

For Discussion

1. How would you feel if you were home all alone one night, and you heard footsteps coming down the hall?

   How would you feel if you looked over and saw Jesus standing in your doorway?

   Do you have anything in your room that you would be embarrassed for him to know about?

2. Do you have anything in your closet that does not really belong to you?

   That you stole?

   If so, what is it?

   What are you going to do with it?

3. Do you have anything in your closet, dresser drawer, or secret hiding place that is morally wrong?

   What is it?

   What are you going to do with it?

11
Our Parents and Our Values

IF we are going to talk about our closets and our own rooms, we might as well go ahead and talk about our parents.

Parents are an emotionally explosive subject. Some teenagers snicker because the subject makes them feel insecure. Some youth get angry and hostile because at home they are in the middle of World War III. Some young people weep because of some inner scar tissue that just won't heal. Many of us have cried ourselves to sleep because of tension within our homes. And most of the arguments are over values.

When I grew up, my parents were strict. I had a 10 o'clock curfew in eleventh grade. It's hard to carry on much of a social life when you need to leave the party at 9:30 P.M.

One evening my dad made me change clothes five times. I got dressed for a party, walked through the kitchen to say good-by, and my dad took one look at my pink shirt, pink pants, and pink shoes and said, "What are you, a girl? Go up and change."

I walked past him a second time wearing jeans, plaid shirt, and boots. "What are you doing, going to a rodeo? Go change."

The third time I wore white pants and a paisley shirt. While I was still walking through the doorway, he said, "What are you, a queer? Go change."

I forgot what it was the fourth time, but the fifth time I was tempted to walk into his closet and pick out something really old-fashioned. Instead, I asked him to come to my closet and pick out my clothes. He loved it!

Essentially, the style clothes we wear has little to do with values. However, parents have much to do with values.

TRADITION

An interesting thing happens when we enter into the teenage years. We begin to test the value system that was handed to us by our parents and our society. Adolescence is a time when we no longer simply plug into someone else's computerized value bank and spit out the answers we've been fed for years. Gradually we begin to challenge traditional values and to ask questions like, "Why?" and "Who says so?" Such rethinking comes not necessarily out of rebellion but out of our need to make deliberate choices of our own personal standard of values. As teenagers moving toward adulthood, we will soon be responsible for all our own actions, and consequently we need values we can sink our teeth into and call our own. Even for those of us who decide to make our parents' values our own, we nonetheless need to make those choices for ourselves.

Parents' values are certainly not infallible. In fact, in certain isolated cases, they are out to lunch. A mother who is an alcoholic can hardly give sound

counsel about self-control. A father who sleeps around or has sexually abused his daughter can hardly teach the value of chastity. Parents who are card-carrying hypocrites are at best negative pictures of what it means to follow Jesus.

However, there are two requirements Jesus makes of every adolescent who has at least one parent still living. As you read this, try to discover what are these two requirements: "Children, obey your parents in the Lord, for this is right. Honor your father and mother—which is the first commandment with a promise—that it may go well with you and that you may enjoy long life on the earth" (Ephesians 6:1–3).

TWO REQUIREMENTS

The first requirement—to obey—is easier. It is the outward action. The second requirement—to honor—is much harder. It involves an internal attitude.

We can obey their request to take out the garbage and yet complain under our breath and even kick the cat out the door.

We can obey their command to study for our history exam while sitting half-asleep with a book in our hands. I heard about one kid whose dad always said to him, "Son, when George Washington was your age, he was getting straight *A*'s." Finally, the kid responded, "Yeah dad, but when he was your age, he was President of the United States."

A girl gets a hat from her grandmother for Christmas. Her mother asks, "Did you thank Nana for the hat?"

"No," the girl replies, "it's an ugly hat."

"But honey," the mother continues, "she's your grandma; thank her anyway."

"Okay," the girl finally concedes. "Thanks, Nana, for the ugly hat!" That's obeying but not honoring. It's going along with the outward action but not the inner attitude.

Hey, I assure you, at times honoring and obeying your parents will not only be frustrating, it will seem foolish. It cuts across the grain. Everything inside just wants to rebel. Even when we decide to choose a strict moral standard, parents can seem to get in the way. "Hey, leave me alone. Give me space! Even if I'm wrong, let me find out for myself." At times we even feel like saying, "Take a hike. Get out of my life for awhile!" It sounds cruel, but there are times when we feel that way.

Then our friends chime in with classic comments like, "Man, your parents sure are strict, from the Dark Ages. I wouldn't put up with that garbage. Don't be a mama's boy. Tell them where to go!" The rock group Twisted Sister had a hit video, "We're Not Gonna Take It," which mocks a parent's authority and encourages open rebellion. On the backside of several Garbage Pail Kids cards, it is printed, "WANTED FOR AGGRAVATED ASSAULT: (Fill in your father's name)"; and "WANTED FOR CHILD ABUSE: (Fill in your mother's name). Also guilty of the following crimes—Aggravated assault by constant nagging; threatening with a deadly weapon—namely 'dad'; throwing away your Garbage Pail Kid stickers."

MURDER IN THE FAMILY

Pedro (name changed) is nineteen. After dinner one night he shot to death his father, mother, and ten-year-old sister. The motive? His father was too strict. Read his confession to the homicide detective:

Detective: Why did you shoot your parents and your sister?

Pedro: I was angry at my father.

Detective: Why?

Pedro: Because he was too strict with me.

Detective: In what way?

Pedro: Every way you can think of.

Detective: Did he ever hit you?

Pedro: Sometimes, but when I was younger, not now.

Detective: You said he was strict, what did he make you do which you thought was strict?

Pedro: I couldn't go out on weekends. I could only go out one day on the weekends. During the week I couldn't do anything. I could see my girlfriend but only one day during the week up until 10:00. And he would make me do a lot of chores I didn't want to do.

Detective: Like what?

Pedro: Like fixing things around the house, washing the car, cleaning the house, painting.

Detective: Did he punish you?

Pedro: Yeah.

Detective: How would he punish you?

Pedro: He would limit the time that I could talk on the phone or take the phone away so I couldn't talk. And I had to be in bed early and I used to have a car which he took away.

When the neighbors had not seen the family for days, they were concerned. When they smelled a suspicious odor, they phoned the police.

Fortunately, not many of us hate our parents with such intensity that we would kill them. However there are times when we treat them like trash. At other times we just ignore them completely, as if they had died.

Perhaps there was more to Pedro's story than the news article reported, but it appeared as though Pedro's father was no stricter than most good parents. At least he appeared no stricter than my father. In fact, even his defense attorneys did not plan to plead insanity because there was not enough evidence of physical or psychological abuse.

The chores Pedro found so burdensome sounded like normal family responsibilities. The punishment which Pedro found so unbearable sounded like the same discipline I received in high school.

The Bible predicted, "In the last days perilous times will come: For men will be lovers of themselves, lovers of money, boasters, proud, blasphemers, disobedient to parents" (2 Timothy 3:1,2 NKJV). It will become a popular trend to tell parents to take a hike and to treat them like excess baggage. However, if we are serious about being followers of Jesus, we don't have that option.

Even in these days when false prophets are lying to our generation about the value of parents and authority, God's promise still stands strong. If we fulfill the two requirements of obeying and honoring our parents, we can claim the promise that goes with them—"that it may go well with you and that you may enjoy long life on the earth."

Let's consider three good reasons for parents: protection, direction, and correction.

1. PARENTS AND PROTECTION

In junior high, a new girl in school came to watch me play football. Whenever I ran the ball or made a tackle, she would scream my name. It didn't take long until the other players started noticing this flurry of attention, especially considering the fact that she was beautiful.

She had long blonde hair. She looked like she was at least eighteen years old. In fact, even my teammates agreed she could have been a Dallas Cowboy cheerleader. But as far as I was concerned, she was my own little personal cheering section. As you can imagine, my teammates were severely jealous, and my ego loved it. She even started coming to our practices to cheer for me.

One day my mother quietly asked me as she picked me up after practice, "Who is that blonde girl you were talking with?"

"Oh, that's Dolly. She is a new girl at school. What a knockout, huh?"

"Well, she thinks you're pretty good." Then she paused and added, "But I don't want you getting interested. She's not your type."

"Not my type!" I gasped. I always thought my mother was a good judge of character. "Mom, everybody in school thinks she's great."

My mother just looked back at me with one of those I'm-not-impressed expressions. It was obvious her mind was made up.

That night the phone rang. It was Dolly. My

first reaction was, *Wow! Wait till my friends hear about this one!"* Then I thought, *What about my mother?* We talked for a while. I hung up, and then my mother walked in. "Who was that?" she asked.

"You know who it was," I said.

"You won't let the relationship develop will you, Fred?" she asked. Against my better judgment, I assured her I wouldn't.

Dolly called a few more times, but I got off the phone sooner each time. Despite the fact that my friends thought I was crazy, and despite the fact that everything inside me was saying, "Go for it," I put my foot on the brakes and got out of the relationship before it even got rolling.

By the end of the school year, bad rumors started circulating about Dolly. She had moral problems. In fact, she never graduated from high school because she got pregnant. Later she married a big-time disc jockey in New York City. She has since been divorced and remarried at least twice.

As a young man all I knew was she looked good on the outside. My mother saw past the surface and knew that inside she did not have the same values I did. By listening to my mother, I was protected from real problems.

When I was growing up, my mother could tell whenever I did something wrong. I couldn't get away with anything. Whenever I did anything wrong, she could take one look at me and know instantly that I was hiding something from her. (Do you have a mother like that?)

I never got into smoking. Maybe I smoked a dozen cigarettes, total. One day after school, I took a few drags on a cigarette at my friend's house. I was so nervous about going home that I showered and gargled with a whole tube of toothpaste. I walked in the back door and strutted like Joe Cool through the kitchen past my mother.

"Fred," she said stopping me in my tracks. Then talking very slowly, emphasizing every word, she asked, "What have you been doing?"

"Oh, nothing, Mom," I said with all the confidence I could gather.

"Fred, come on, I know you've done something wrong. Now tell me the truth. What was it?"

I couldn't believe it! How did she know? I had no choice. I told her.

I never got very interested in pornography, but I did look at three magazines—three more than I wish I had seen. One day I ripped a picture out of a friend's magazine. It was 1″ x 1″, about the size of a postage stamp. I folded it six or seven times and tucked it in the bottom of my sock. I snuck through the house, up into the attic, and hid it under a layer of insulation.

When I came downstairs for a snack, my mother took one look at me and said, "Fred, I know you've been into something." Caught again!

I never did figure out how she could do that, but I have discovered that thousands of other young people throughout the country have mothers just like mine. You know why? The Bible tells us:

My son, keep your father's commands and do not forsake your mother's teaching. Bind them upon your heart forever; fasten them around your neck. When you walk, they will guide you; when you sleep, they will watch over you; when you awake, they will speak to you. For these commands are a lamp, this teaching is a light, and the corrections of discipline are the way to life (Proverbs 6:20–23).

2. PARENTS AND DIRECTION

When we start making big-time decisions like where to go to college, who to marry, what career to pursue, where to live, advice from our parents is extremely valuable. It is valuable even when it seems like a drag.

Joan was sixteen years old, lived in Fort Myers, Florida, and was full of enthusiasm for Jesus. Her parents were nominal Christians and hardly went to church. When they told her she could no longer attend the teen Bible study, she went bananas. To her, it was as if they asked her to forsake Christ.

At a Tuesday night Bible study she showed up in tears. After we settled her down, she explained the situation. We asked her how she got there if they refused to let her attend any longer. "I climbed out the window," she admitted.

The youth group immediately prayed for Joan, and then I gave her a proposal. "Hey, let's try an experiment. You stay home. Do everything they tell you—vacuum, do dishes, all your chores. Then when you're done with those, do extra things around the house they don't even ask you to do. Once in a while explain to them, with a smile, that the reason you are obeying and honoring them is because they are God's appointed authority over you."

She listened for a while, then wrapped her face in her hands, and sobbed more, "But, I'll never attend church again. . . ."

I gave her three verses:

Children, obey your parents in the Lord, for this is right. Honor your father and mother—which is the first commandment with a promise—that it may go well with you and that you may enjoy long life on the earth (Ephesians 6:1-3).

The king's heart is in the hand of the Lord; he directs it like a watercourse wherever he pleases (Proverbs 21:1)

When a man's ways are pleasing to the Lord, he makes even his enemies live at peace with him (Proverbs 16:7).

She settled down. We prayed. She agreed to try it, and we all committed ourselves to pray for her every day.

She went home and immediately started showing love to her parents in tangible ways.

A few weeks later the phone rang. "Fred, I'm so excited!" It was Joan. "It is wonderful. My dad wants the whole youth group to come over and have a pool party this Friday night. He said we can even study the Bible. Can you come?"

We not only went, we had a great time. Before we left their home, we stood in a circle to hold hands and pray. Joan's dad walked in and interrupted, "Hey, what's going on?" I looked at Joan, and she looked like she wished she could climb out the window again. Embarrassed bad.

"We are just talked to Jesus. You want to join us?"

"Sure, why not?" He not only joined hands with us, but he prayed. "Hey, God, I think this is great these kids are talking to You like this. They are really great, you know what I mean, God? Amen." Nobody could believe it. Joan's dad prayed.

He not only prayed that night, but the whole family was in church the next Sunday. In fact, a month later the whole family was baptized together.

Joan not only learned how important it is to honor and obey her parents during high school, but it helped her discover God's will during college. While Joan wanted to pursue a missionary career, her parents wanted her to go into nursing. She ended up marrying a young man her parents approved of—a doctor—and they are currently serving as a medical team overseas. That's exciting!

3. PARENTS AND CORRECTION

We like making decisions for ourselves. We do not like people telling us what to do, even when those people are our parents. We want the responsibility to decide . . .

▶ How loud to play our music.
▶ Which friends we hang around with.
▶ What time we get home.
▶ Where we work.
▶ How we spend our money.
▶ How we spend our time.
▶ The way we wear our hair.
▶ What clothes we wear.
▶ What car we drive.

▸ What college we attend.
▸ What career we pursue.
▸ Whom we marry.

While we wrestle for control over all these responsibilities, we need to understand that correction is still part of our parents' responsibility. They do it out of love.

A missionary kid in the Congo was playing one afternoon behind his house. Suddenly, he heard his dad's voice yell, "Son, obey me immediately. Drop to your stomach." The boy obeyed.

"Now crawl towards me as fast as you can." Again he obeyed.

"Now stand and run to me." The boy ran into his father's arms. The father then turned the boy around and pointed to the branch over the area where he had been standing. Hanging from the branch was a deadly fifteen-foot snake. There had been no time for delay. No time for debate. If the boy had argued, "But Dad, I'm having too much fun. Can't I come in later?", it might have been too late. The father gave the command because he loved his son, and the son was preserved because he obeyed his father's command.

We were vacationing in Maine. My son, Fred, and I walked into a drugstore, and while standing at the checkout counter he asked me, "Dad, can I have this pack of gum?" The answer was, "No," so he asked again. "Aw, Dad, please." The gum was imported from Sweden and cost $1.25. I again said, "No," this time a bit more forcefully.

The woman behind the counter got involved, "What's the matter, Dad? Don't you love him?"

I admit I didn't care for her questions, but you should have seen Fred. He stood on his tiptoes, grabbed the counter, looked her in the face, and said in full voice to my defense, "Yes, he loves me! That's why he doesn't give me everything I ask for!" It blew the lady away.

I hope Fred always remembers that principle.

MAKE A DATE

During the summer of my senior year of high school, I was busy. I worked eight hours a day, was on a softball team, had a girlfriend, and attended a weekly Bible study, so I was gone most of the time.

I grabbed a piece of chicken as I walked through the kitchen and yelled "See you later, Mom and Dad."

"Where are you going?" my dad asked.

"I got a date with Susan."

"Hey Fred," my dad asked as I reached the back door, "some night can I have a date with you?" Wow! It was like he knocked the wind out of me. I let the screen door swing shut, and it hit me in the face. I hung my head in regret. Here I had learned to submit to my parents, and they gave me many freedoms. Yet I had been neglecting them.

That night I decided that since I would be leaving for college in the fall, every week that summer I would make a date with them. Once a week I spent an evening with them, and once a month I took them out for dinner.

Cornell University did a test that involved strapping recording mechanisms to small preschool children. It was determined that the average father of a child in that age group spent 37.7 seconds a day in interaction.

The National PTA has determined that the average teenager spends 7.5 minutes a week in meaningful conversation with his parents. How much meaningful conversation can you have in 7.5 minutes?

Gallup pollsters surveyed 1,000 teenagers and discovered 25 percent do not discuss their daily activities with their parents. Forty-two percent did not hear their parents say a single positive word in the previous twenty-four hours. Half had not received a hug or kiss, and 54 percent had not heard the words, "I love you." Seventy-nine percent said their parents no longer helped them with their homework.

DADDY! DADDY!

Tuesday morning, January 28, 1986, Allison Smith got up early, put on warm clothes, and went out to Cape Kennedy Space Center to watch her daddy take off in the shuttle. He was the pilot, Michael Smith.

It was a beautiful morning. The air was clear and crisp. She got excited when the countdown started: "10-9-8-7-...." Everyone was cheering. The rockets were ignited. The shuttle lifted off. Everything appeared flawless. Pride swept through the crowd.

Then came the horrible sight we all watched replay after replay. Slightly more than a minute after takeoff, the shuttle blew up. People gasped. Silence. Then a child's voice cut through the air, "Daddy, Daddy, I want you, Daddy. You always promised nothing would happen." Silence. No answer came back, just the harsh, cold reality that her daddy was gone. Her daddy would never answer another question. How would you feel if you were Allison Smith, and your daddy was gone?

I met a guy from California whose dad died when he was twelve, and he said he'd been bitter ever since. He was six feet tall and at least two hundred pounds, with tears running down his face. I shared with him Psalm 68:5, "God is a father of the fatherless, a defender of widows" (NKJV). "Dan," I said to him, "in a special way, you have greater capacity to understand God's love and compassion. He doesn't leave you without a father. He is your Father, and He lets you know His love so much more."

We talked for a while and then prayed. Two days later he told me that for the first time in seven years, he was free from his anger.

A kid in New Jersey had a very smart father. The dad had cancer and knew he had only three months to live, and so he wrote his son a series of letters. He sealed them in separate envelopes, marked them appropriately, and gave them to an anonymous friend with careful instructions.

Eight months after the father died, the boy was feeling sad and sorry for himself because his birthday was coming up. When he checked the mailbox, he found one envelope he opened very quickly. It was from his dad. He couldn't believe his eyes. He read something like this.

Dear Son,
    I am now in heaven and we don't get to

see each other anymore but I want you to know that I think a lot about you, too. I know you will be 14 this week so I wanted to wish you a happy birthday and tell you, you don't have to feel sorry for me—I'm better off here. And you don't have to feel sorry for yourself either. Jesus is right there with you all the time.

Son, that's what I wanted to talk with you about. You see, son, you're getting older now and you need to assume responsibility.

You always wanted to make decisions for yourself. Now you probably make more than you hoped for. I'm not there to help you make those decisions anymore but you know a lot of people thought I was a wise man and I know you always thought I was pretty special. So as you're making decisions I want to give you a tip. Just ask yourself, "What would my dad do if he was here?" And if that doesn't help, ask, "What would Jesus do if He was here?"

Son, I'm sure the world is not getting any better. I'm sure living straight isn't any easier on you. But I'll tell you something, son. If you live right down there and make the right choices, when you get up here with me you will never regret it.

Son, I can't wait to see you.

Your Daddy

If your dad is still living, don't treat him as if he was dead. Don't neglect either of your parents.

I can guarantee you that neither your mom nor your dad is perfect, but that doesn't disqualify them from being your parents. They didn't have to take some exam in order to earn the right to be your parents. When you were born, God gave you to them as a gigantic responsibility. God holds them accountable to do a good job raising you, especially in the three key areas—protection, direction, and correction. And God holds us accountable to receive from them.

The next year prior to his birthday, the boy in New Jersey went to the mailbox every day to see if there was a letter. Sure enough, one day it came. Every year he got a letter, and then one final letter the month prior to his wedding day, just as his daddy had planned.

Parents can't punch our buttons and program our computer with their values. But neither can we cruise through life thinking we don't need their help as we choose our values. Ultimately, our values come from the Bible, but if we let them, our parents can sure help us in the process.

When was the last time you told your parents that you love them?

For Discussion

1. Are you able to talk freely to your parents? Why or why not?

2. What areas of your life are difficult to talk about with your parents?

3. Do your parents trust you?
   Why or why not?

4. What do you and your parents argue about?
   Make a list.

5. On a scale of 1 to 10 (10 being the strictest), rank your mom.
   Rank your dad.

6. Is it healthy to challenge our parents value system?

7. Are our parents always right?
   Are they usually right?
   How should we respond when they are wrong?

8. What two responsibilities do we have toward our parents?

9. How can parents benefit us?

10. List the qualities of a perfect mother
    List the qualities of a perfect father.
    Read the lists to your parents.
    Ask them to make a similar list describing a perfect son or daughter.

11. Why might it be a good idea to "date our parents?"

12
Full Speed Ahead

AFTER midnight, Stephen sat on the edge of his parents' bed. With tears running down his cheeks, he told them everything. He told them about all the garbage he had been involved in. Then together they told God about it. After hugging each other and reaffirming their love and respect for each other, Stephen's dad asked him a probing question, "Did you repent just to feel better about yourself, or because you really hate sin and genuinely want to please Christ?"

"No, Dad," Stephen answered, "I really believe that I am serious about serving the Lord. I know I have a lot to learn, and I have a long way to go, but I am ready to start moving in the right direction."

That was two months ago, and since then Stephen and his dad have met consistently once a week to study the Bible, pray, and talk together about following Jesus. It is obvious that Stephen not only turned from evil but has aggressively started doing good.

Yesterday Stephen called and asked me, "Is

there anything I can do to serve the Lord around the church? Just let me know."

It's not every day I get a phone call like that. But I am sure God will give Stephen some challenging assignments as he desires to please Jesus.

When we repent of our old lifestyle of rebellion and self-interest, it is time for us to sink our teeth into our new way of life. "If anyone is in Christ, he is a new creation; the old has gone, the new has come!" (2 Corinthians 5:17). Rather than mourning the death of our old way of life, we need to celebrate our new life in Jesus.

Repentance is twofold. "Turn from evil and do good" (Psalm 37:27). Simply to turn from evil is boring because it is only half a life. When we start to do good, that is when things become exciting.

MOTHBALL CHRISTIANS

The United States Navy has 768 ships that comprise what is known as the "mothball navy." These ships are anchored in various harbors around the country. They receive regular maintenance to ensure combat readiness on a moment's notice, but on a day-to-day basis they do absolutely nothing.

I wonder how large a fleet we have of "mothball Christians"—people who call themselves followers of Christ, yet who just sit and do absolutely nothing. They are smugly anchored in various churches and youth groups. They require lots of pampering from concerned friends and consume incredible amounts of time and energy. Yet they themselves never lift a finger to serve anyone else. Oh, they

might pass the offering plates, erase the chalk-boards, sit in the nursery, or twiddle thumbs for Jesus, but they rarely put forth much effort, and they never sacrifice.

I can see a legitimate reason for maintaining our mothball navy. Our national security requires it. Yet there is no reason for mothball Christians. There is a whole world to reach with the gospel, and we need all hands on deck. It's time to push out from our safe harbors and start serving others.

GOOD FOR NOTHING

Another problem develops when we clean up our act yet never explain that the reason is Jesus. Our friends know that we are different. They know we don't smoke grass, we don't have sex, we don't get drunk. From their perspective, we look upside down. But they don't know why. They know we're good, but they think we're just good for nothing.

Being *good for nothing* doesn't make sense to anyone. It doesn't ring true. In fact, being good for nothing is a lie. No one is just good for nothing.

The only way our lives will ever make sense to an upside-down generation is to explain the difference. Rather than just being good for nothing, we need to explain that we are being *good for Jesus*. The time has come for us not to go to school simply as students; we need to go to school as missionaries. We need to communicate that the reason we dance to the beat of a different music is because we have a different set of values, and the reason we have a different set of values is because we belong to Jesus.

OLD FRIENDS

I get tired of parents' blaming their teenager's behavior on their teenager's friends. The problem is usually not with their kid's friends—it's with their kids. We look for friends who enjoy the same things we do. So if a young person would no longer hang around with a friend his parents disapprove of, he would most likely find another friend similar to the first. As the saying goes, "Birds of a feather flock together." Instead of parents' pointing the finger at the kid down the street, they would do better to deal with the one in the bedroom down the hall.

While it is true that we cannot blame our behavior on our friends, once we repent and change our value system, it is important for us to recognize something. For the first time there is a radical difference between ourself and our old friends. Our friends are no different. They are no better or worse than they used to be, and we can't expect them to be any different. But *we* are different, and we are the ones who need to be unashamedly and uncompromisingly honest about the difference. Without embarrassment to ourself or our friends, we need to draw the line and say, "Hey, my life now belongs to Jesus, and I can't do that any more." If we don't learn to say that, we will never survive as a follower of Jesus in our generation.

The Bible does say, "Do not be misled: Bad company corrupts good character. Come back to your senses as you ought, and stop sinning" (1 Corinthians 15:33–34). While we need to assume responsibility for our own actions rather than blaming our friends, there comes a time when some relationships will shrivel up and die.

A kid in New England who was one of the best drummers in the high-school marching band was recently kicked out because he was not keeping step with the rest of the band. It was discovered he was wearing a set of FM earphones under his hat and was actually listening to music from hundreds of miles away. No wonder he couldn't keep in step with those around him.

If we want to be in the school band, we need to keep step with everyone else. However, when we're not in the school band, Jesus does not want us to keep step with everyone else. He wants us to wear our heavenly earphones and to be tuned into His station, which comes from outer space. Then we will seem out of step, and we might lose friends, but it is only because we're dancing to different music. At first, friends might mock and laugh, but then some might even start dancing with us.

THE REASON FOR THE DIFFERENCE

In my high school, my friends knew me as a straight kid. Some even knew I was a Christian, but I never told anyone how they could receive Jesus as their Savior and Lord.

Like many Christian kids, I was very guilty about my silence. One Sunday night at church, the minister preached a ripsnorting message about telling others about Jesus. He quoted the verse, "I am not ashamed of the gospel, because it is the power of God for the salvation of everyone who believes" (Romans 1:16).

I went to school Monday morning psyched-up to tell people how to get to heaven. I sat in the library and prayed, *Jesus, the first guy to sit next to me, I will tell him about You.* Just then my best friend walked into the room. *Oh, no! Lord, You can't do this to me!* I panicked. *Have him sit at another table, Lord. Please? Anybody but him, Lord.*

Before I was done pleading, my best friend sat down next to me. I froze. I couldn't even say, "good morning." Ten minutes later the bell rang, and it was time to go to our first period class. I felt sick to my stomach. I was disgusted with myself. I told God I felt like a failure, but I asked Him for a second chance.

Then a great idea popped into my head. God gave me a great icebreaker to start a conversation with my old friends about Jesus.

Here it is: *I've known you for a long time, but I've never told you about the most important thing in my life. May I tell you about it?*

It was honest. It was right to the point. And how could anyone say no?

I called my friend Dave. I was nervous, but I said, "Dave, I've known you for a long time, but I've never told you about the most important thing in my life. May I tell you about it?"

He said something I'll never forget. "Fred, I always knew there was something different about you that never made sense before. I've been waiting for you to tell me about it."

At first I felt rebuked, but then after I read him a couple of verses from the Bible and explained what Jesus meant to me, I sure felt relieved. I told Dave about Jesus, and now he knew the reason for the difference in my life.

For me, that was an important turning point.

From that day I was no longer just a straight kid. I was Christ's kid. I was no longer a mothball Christian. I moved from a half-repentance to a whole repentance. Not only did I flee evil, but I started to do good. It was only a beginning, but for the first time in my life, I felt like I was part of God's team. It felt so good that there was no turning back.

THE LADY WHO LOOKED BACK

One of the weirdest stories in the Bible is about a lady who was suddenly forced to move from her home. She was warned that God was about to drop an atomic bomb on the city in which she lived, and she and her entire family were told to evacuate immediately. Otherwise, they would get scorched with the rest of the crowd. We are not even told the lady's name, but she was married to a guy named Lot. As she and her family packed a few suitcases and headed for the hills, God gave them one more strict warning, "Don't look back! Whatever you do, when I drop the bomb, don't look back."

When she and her family were at a safe distance from the city, it exploded into flames. Everyone else in her family hid their faces and refused to look back, but this poor gal couldn't resist. All she wanted was a little peek.

She'd lived there for years. Many of her friends were going up in flames. And after all, she had obeyed God by leaving. *What harm could there be if I just took a little peek?* she thought.

Instantly, as the sight of the burning city hit her eyeballs, her eyes froze in their sockets. Her lungs filled. Her heart hardened. Her brain died. In fact, her flesh immediately decomposed, and she mysteriously turned into a human saltshaker. She became a hunk of sodium silicoaluminate right on the spot. Yikes! That story blows my mind! (Read Genesis 19 for the original account.)

I never understood why God was so hard on that lady, even though the city of Sodom in which she lived was a horribly immoral place. Recently, however, I have realized that she is an example to us not to look back fondly at the things God has condemned.

Jesus said, "No one who puts his hand to the plow and looks back is fit for service in the Kingdom of God" (Luke 9:62).

Once we leave the city of sin and the lifestyle that goes with it, we are better off not looking back. Once we set our hand to the plow and commit ourselves to serve Jesus, we don't need to reconsider the options.

It is good to reaffirm the verses of the simple chorus, "I Have Decided to Follow Jesus":

> I have decided to follow Jesus,
>   . . . No turning back.
> The world behind me, the cross before
>   me,
>   . . . No turning back.
> Tho none go with me, I still will follow,
>   . . . No turning back.
> Will you decide now to follow Jesus?
>   . . . No turning back.

Full speed ahead!

For Discussion

1. Define *mothball Christian.*
Have you ever known one?

2. Why did the lady turn into salt?
What does this story teach us?

3. Why are we sometimes embarrassed to talk about Jesus?
Have you ever been embarrassed to talk about Jesus?
Describe the feeling.
How did you deal with it?

4. If we are straight because we are Christians, why should we tell our friends about Jesus?

13

Semper Fi

WHEN it is all said and done, when the band quits playing and the lights go out and the party is over, the only thing that will really matter is *Did I do what He told me to do?*

A few years ago, we were awakened early one Sunday morning by the horrifying news that a fanatical terrorist drove a truck through barricades in Beirut, Lebanon. He smashed into the front lobby of an apartment building that housed hundreds of our marines. The impact detonated explosives in the truck and devastated the entire structure. The figures came back slowly as the bodies were being found—70, 90, 147, 204, 225 dead!

Most Americans looked on and said, "What are we doing there anyway?" And virtually the entire world looked on and said, "What a waste! What a waste of fine young men."

Later that same week from a medical ward in Europe came a report that touched the hearts of people everywhere. Marine commandant Paul Kelly was making the rounds to present the honorary medal, the Purple Heart, to each of the survivors. He walked into the room of one badly injured young marine who was bandaged from head to foot with tubes sticking from various parts of his body. The commandant identified himself, but since the young man could not see because of the bandages, he motioned with his protruding hand for the commandant to bend down so that the marine might touch the stars on his shoulder to verify that he was the commandant.

The commandant obliged. After touching the stars, the marine, unable to talk since his mouth was partially wired shut, motioned for a piece of paper. On it he scribbled the words *semper fi*—the Marine abbreviation for the Latin term *semper fidelis*, which means "always faithful."

At that moment the young marine, who all but gave his life, expressed no regrets, no complaints, no sense of loss. At that moment he reaffirmed his commitment to fulfill his duty, no matter what the cost.

It is time for us as Christians to decide if Jesus and His gospel are worth the sacrifice. Hey, the tongues of outsiders will always wag against anyone who sacrifices, and they will say, "What a waste! What a waste!" But, you see, outsiders don't make sacrifices.

You can determine a person's value system according to what they are willing to sacrifice and what they are not willing to sacrifice. When someone with one set of values looks at someone sacrificing because of a different set of values, they will always say, "What a waste."

To sacrifice is *to give up something of value in order to gain something of greater value.* An insider who sacrifices looks only at the greater value he is

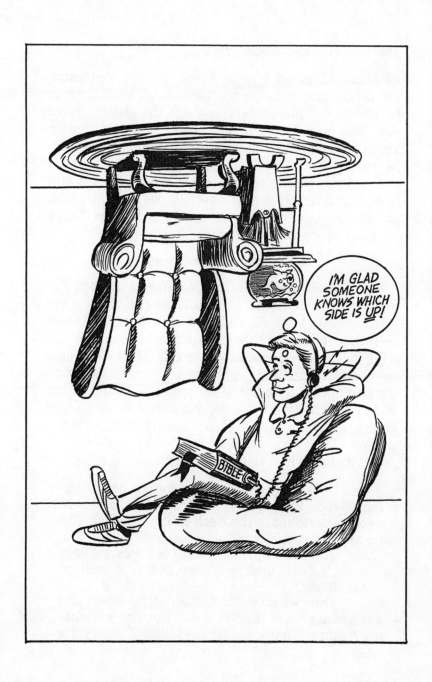

gaining. When my marine friend met his command-
ing officer, nothing else mattered other than that he
had been faithful in carrying out the orders given.
Any loss he suffered in the process did not matter,
since he had pleased the one giving the orders.
Semper fi!

Once we are completely sold out to Jesus and
fully enlist ourselves in His service, we no longer look
at the things we have to give up. We look at the things
we gain which are of much greater value.

HOORAY FOR BUBBA SMITH!

Cheers were familiar to Bubba Smith. For
years in the National Football League, Bubba enjoyed playing football, and the fans loved him. When
he retired, he needed something else to do, and he hit
it big in TV ads—especially beer ads. Most of us have
watched him rip the tops off cans. When he threw up
the flag and said he would no longer do beer ads, nobody could believe it. Think of all the money he was
giving up. Many said, "What a waste!" Well, was it a
waste?

Let's let him tell us the story.

I went back to Michigan State for the homecom-
ing parade last year. I was the grand marshall
and I was riding in the back seat of this car. The
people were yelling, but they weren't saying, "Go,
State, go!" One side of the street was yelling,
"Tastes great!" and the other side was yelling,
"Less filling."

Then we go to the stadium. The older folks
are yelling, "Kill, Bubba, kill!" But the students
are yelling, "Tastes great! Less filling!" Everyone

in the stands is drunk. It was like I was contribut-
ing to alcohol, and I don't drink. It made me realize I was doing something I didn't want to do.

I was with my brother Tody, who is my
agent. I told him, "Tody, I'll never do another Lite
beer commercial." He almost——on himself.

At that same time, Bubba Smith and his
brother were working through a contract with a beer
brewery. Bubba stuck to his convictions and said no.

The beer people thought it was because of
the money. But it didn't have nothing to do with
the money. That was hard to give up, especially
me, being a black athlete, it's hard to get stuff
[commercial endorsements].

I loved doing the commercials, but I didn't
like the effect it was having on a lot of little people. I'm talking about people in school. Kids
would come up to me on the street and recite
lines from my commercials, verbatim. They knew
the lines better than I did. It was scary. [When]
kids start to listen to things you say, you want to
tell 'em something that is the truth.

Doing those commercials, it's like me telling everyone in school, hey, it's cool to have a Lite
beer. I'd go to places like Daytona Beach and
Fort Lauderdale on spring breaks as a spokesman for the brewery, and it was scary to see how
drunk those kids were. It was fun talking to the
fans, until you see people lying on the beach because they can't make it back to their room, or
tearing up a city.

As the years wear on, you stop compro-
mising yours principles.

Bubba Smith, I clap for you! You didn't slow down the sales of beer. From what I understand, rather than picturing you ripping off the lids of beer cans, they picked L. C. Greenwood—another intimidating, black, former pro-football player—to rip trees out of the ground. However, you did take a stand. You were true to your convictions and wouldn't compromise, even though it cost you a lot of money. You sacrificed, but it was not a waste. You gave up something of value, but you gained something of far greater value—integrity.

Bubba Smith demonstrated a very important principle we all need to learn. In this life there is nothing more important than being authentic—being open and honest about who we are and what values we hold. Once we claim our values, we need to cling to them and refuse to compromise them, no matter what the cost.

IS JESUS WORTH IT?

We can be Christians and regret it. We can live on the fringe of His love, and yet still be in the circle. We can try to walk as far out on the edge as we can without stepping out.

But a wonderful thing happens when we come to the place in our lives with Jesus when we no longer ask, "What can I *get away with* and still be a Christian?" Instead, we start asking, "What can I *give up* to be a better Christian?" Following Jesus gets very exciting when we stop saying, "You mean, I *have* to . . ." and start saying, "You mean I *get* to. . . ?"

I can't tell you when that happens. Sometimes it is only a subtle shift in attitude, but it makes light-years of difference. We no longer follow Jesus because someone else told us to; we start following Jesus because it is the only thing we want to do.

One day Jesus made a statement that blew a few minds. (He was famous for making statements like that.) Several of His followers couldn't handle it, and so they gave up. They quit. Then Jesus turned to the rest of His disciples and asked, "You do not want to leave too, do you?" (John 6:67).

Peter became the spokesman and said, "Lord, to whom shall we go? You have the words of eternal life" (v. 68).

I like that. I like it because Jesus shows here that He always gives us the option. He does not grab our lives from us. He does not force us to follow. He doesn't expect us to go through the motions when our hearts aren't in it. I also like it because Peter hit the nail on the head. He clearly indicated that as far as he was concerned, there were no other options. His mind was made up. He wasn't following Jesus out of duty, but rather out of choice. He knew he was free, but He chose to follow Jesus because Jesus was worth it.

Is Jesus worth it to you?

THE PRICE HE PAID

Lester (name changed) is thirteen years old and lives in Orlando, Florida. One Friday he woke up at 2:00 A.M. choking on smoke. He jumped up and ran out of the house. As he looked back, he saw the flames and had a sick feeling in his stomach as he realized his house was burning down. He looked around and saw his dad and mom. He started screaming when he realized his two kid brothers were still inside. There was no time to wait for anyone else to do something about it, so he ran back through the flames into their bedroom. He wrapped them in a bedspread and ran back through the flames carrying them over his shoulder. He collapsed outside the house.

His brothers were fine except for a little smoke inhalation, but Lester was rushed to the hospital with second-degree burns on his hands and face. When he regained the consciousness, the first thing he asked was, "How are my brothers?" He will survive and will certainly be a hero to his brothers, but doctors assume he will have permanent scars.

You and I were in a house of destruction. We faced eternal fire and death and judgment. There was nothing we could do to escape. We would have slept our way into hell, and then it would have been too late. Jesus was the only One who could help. He ran in through the flames, wrapped us in His love, picked us up in His arms, and carried us through the flames. But in rescuing us, He died in the process. He gave His life so that we might live forever.

Rather than being taken to the hospital, He was taken to the cemetery and buried. Everyone gave up on Him—everyone but His Father. Three days after He died, His Father raised Him from the dead. Today Jesus lives to save us from the house of destruction and from the eternal flames. Can we say that about anyone else?

As Jesus hung on the cross dying for us, there were certainly people looking on saying, "What a waste. What a fine young man. He had so much potential. It's too bad He had to die. He could have done so much good for so many people. What a waste."

You see, as we look at Jesus hanging from the cross, there are really only two options. Either we say, *"What a waste,"* or we say, *"You alone are worthy. You alone deserve my loyalty, my service, my devotion."* Either Christ is worth more than everything or He is not worth anything.

What do you say?

A WASTE

You want to know what a *waste* is?

- A *waste* is a Christian with an upside-down value system.
- A *waste* is a young person with a whole life to give to Jesus who instead says, "Maybe when I'm older."
- A *waste* is someone called to live for Jesus and contribute to an eternal kingdom but who spends his time and energies on the little things of this world.
- A *waste* is anyone who puts off getting right with God.
- A *waste* is someone who cares more about what other people think than what Jesus thinks.

On Tuesday, January 28, 1986, when the shuttle Challenger exploded soon after lift-off, we wept. Replay after replay, our hearts felt worse and worse because of the loss of life and because of the aborted mission.

But it hurts me even worse to think about all

the young lives that are aborted and never reach their God-given potential because they settle for the puny pleasures of sin. When Jesus speaks to us and calls us, it is time to respond.

Catherine Booth of the Salvation Army told one young person, "Young woman, you have not the right to waste your life."

When we compromise our convictions to avoid personal embarrassment, we sell ourselves short. When we clean up our act but don't tell anyone the reason, we might be good, but we're good-for-nothing. When we put a premium on our reputations and do anything our friends expect just to avoid rejection, we are wasting our potential, and our lives will never have an impact on anyone. The One who really loses in all this is Jesus, who gave His life for us.

The only way we will ever make a difference in our generation is by daring to be different.

RUNNING WITH THE WIND

"Chariots of Fire," winner of four Academy Awards including "Best Picture," is my favorite movie. Essentially it is a study in character and values. The film focuses on the life of a restless Hebrew college student at Cambridge University in England, who competes against Eric Liddle, a Christian with high moral values.

Liddle is my hero. His father told him, "The Kingdom of God is not a democracy. . . . God doesn't get reelected every year. . . . There is one right and one wrong . . . one Absolute Law." He also said, "Don't compromise. Compromise is the devil's language. . . .

Run in God's name and let the world stand back and watch."

According to Liddle's convictions, it is wrong to run on Sundays. As the Bible says, "Remember the Sabbath day by keeping it holy" (Exodus 20:8). When he learned that the Olympic qualifying heat for his race—the 100 meters—was on Sunday, he was faced with a major decision. *Do I run and lower my convictions or hold to my convictions and lose the opportunity to run in the Olympics?* His decision would reveal his values. Even though he was saddened, he never flinched. His decision? "I will not run!"

The Prince of Wales tried to pressure Liddle to change his mind. A member of the English Olympic Committee asked, "Just how far does your arrogance extend?" Liddle's response was classic. "My arrogance extends just as far as my conscience demands." I love it!

After the decision was made, even the Prince affirmed, "This Liddle is a man of principle; you can't sever his running from the man." He was correct. The leg strength of Eric Liddle the runner was intimately connected to the moral strength of Eric Liddle the Christian. If he compromised one, he would lose the other.

The drama peaked as another British runner, who had already won a silver medal, yielded his position in the 400 meters, allowing Liddle a chance to run. Everyone realized it was a long shot since Liddle had trained for the 100 meters, a considerably shorter race.

Prior to the final race, an American runner handed Liddle words from the Old Testament scribbled on a piece of paper, "Those who honor me, I will honor."

Clutching that promise in his hand, Liddle bent down at the starting blocks with the other runners. The gun cracked! They took off. Liddle gave it everything he had. His legs pumped like pistons. His arms driving. His lungs sucked hard. Every tendon was as tight as a piano string. Liddle never looked back. His eyes were focused on the finish line like heat-seeking missiles. When he broke the tape and won the gold, the crowd went crazy.

Liddle not only had guts, but his uncompromising convictions put him in a class all by himself. Every time I watch the movie, I can't help but bow my head and ask *where are all the runners who run like that? Where are the moral pacesetters?*

TWO ROADS

Growing up is a series of life-changing decisions.

▸ Which college (or no college)?
▸ Which career?
▸ Which marriage partner (or no marriage partner)?

Robert Frost's famous poem, "The Road Not Taken," talks about a fork in the road and the consequences that follow when we choose one road and reject the other. We usually do not have the opportunity to retrace our steps to explore the alternative road we rejected. The fork in the road represents our decision.

Of all the decisions we have to make in life, the most significant is our value system. In our society there are four major value systems:

1. *Humanistic.* Man is of ultimate value; whatever is good for man is the highest good.
2. *Materialistic.* Things (money, possessions) are of ultimate value; whatever enables me to accumulate wealth is the highest good.
3. *Hedonistic.* Pleasure is of ultimate value; whatever satisfies my appetites is the highest good.
4. *Christian.* Christ is of ultimate value; whatever brings glory to Him is the highest good.

One of the first men to choose the fourth alternative was Paul the apostle. He uncompromisingly stated, "For to me, to live is Christ and to die is gain" (Philippians 1:21).

▸ For an athlete, to live is a cheering crowd.
▸ For an alcoholic, to live is a bottle of bourbon.
▸ For a drug addict, to live is a heroin needle.
▸ For a surfer, to live is the perfect wave.
▸ For a Christian, to live is Christ.

Christianity stands alone as a value system because all the rest are self-centered. Essentially, choosing a value system is choosing between two roads. I will either spend my life living for myself, or I will spend it living for the One who made me. Paul chose the road less traveled, and it made all the difference for him. Choosing Christ will make all the difference for anyone who breaks loose from other upside-down values.

WHAT OUR GENERATION NEEDS

Every school and neighborhood needs a pacesetter, a leader, someone who dances to the beat of a different drum. Like never before, our generation needs young people with enough courage to draw the line and refuse to step over it; individuals who have moral convictions they refuse to compromise regardless of what other people think; men and women who base their values, not on the shifting sand of popular opinion, but on the eternal standard of God's Word. Any old dead fish can float downstream. It takes a live one to go against the flow.

It's too late for neutrality. The gap is widening. We can't pretend to be a friend of God while we try desperately to be a friend of this upside-down world. It's time to choose sides.

Toward the end of his life, the great leader Moses challenged the next generation, "This day I call heaven and earth as witnesses against you that I have set before you life and death, blessing and curses. Now choose life, so that you and your children may live and that you may love the Lord your God, listen to his voice and hold fast to him. For the Lord is your life" (Deuteronomy 30:19–20).

One of the young men who accepted the challenge was Joshua, who also became a great leader of God's people. Toward the end of his life, he in turn challenged the next generation: "But if serving the Lord seems undesirable to you, then choose for yourselves this day whom you will serve" (Joshua 24:15).

The world has enough copycats, robots, plastic people, look-alikes and tagalongs. What the world needs is more originals—more authentic people who insist on walking straight in an upside-down world. There are enough blind prophets leading blind peo-

ple off cliffs. We need more mountain climbers whose
sights are set on the finish line of heaven. We need
more radical Christians with the goal of one day looking face-to-face at Commandant Christ and simply
saying, *semper fi*. At that moment we will receive all
the reward we need when we hear Him say, "Well
done, good and faithful servant!" (Matthew 25:23).

For Discussion

1. Define *hero*.
   What qualities make a person a hero?

2. Whom do you respect?
   Why?

3. Define *sacrifice*.

4. What does Bubba Smith teach us about values?
   About sacrifice?

5. Thirteen-year-old Lester ran in a burning house to
   save his brothers.
   How does Lester resemble Jesus?

6. What does it mean to dance to the beat of a different drummer?

7. What does the film *Chariots of Fire* teach us about values?

8. Define the differences between a Christian value system and any other value system.

9. What is the highest value in your life?

Appendix A

Famous Quotes from Famous People on Values

President Ronald Reagan: The good Lord who has given our country so much should never have been expelled from our nation's classrooms. . . . A value-neutral education is a contradiction in terms. The American people have always known in their bones how intimately knowledge and values are intertwined. If we give our children no guidance here, we are robbing them of their most precious inheritance—the wisdom of generations that is contained in our moral heritage.

—Weekly radio broadcast, Santa Barbara, California

Billy Graham: That leaves our young people with absolutely no trusted source of moral guidelines. Millions are simply making it up as they go along. They stumble into the future without a moral compass to guide them. . . . I find that youth want moral guidelines. They want to be told with authority what is right and what is wrong. . . . Prominently display . . . in every schoolroom in America . . . the Ten Commandments. I don't see how any Jew, Catholic or Protestant could object to letting our young people know we believe in something.

—*Miami Herald*, May 8, 1985

President Theodore Roosevelt: The things that will destroy America are prosperity at any price, peace at any price, safety first instead of duty first, a love of soft living and the "get rich" theory of life.

President George Washington: Morality and religion are the two pillars of our society.

Dr. James Dobson: We are involved in nothing less than a civil war of values—a collision between two ways of seeing life.

—*Focus on the Family* magazine,
March 1985

Steven Muller, President of Johns Hopkins University: The biggest failing in higher education today is that we fall short in exposing students to values. . . . This situation has come about because the modern university is rooted in the scientific method, having essentially turned its back on religion. . . . It has taken a long time for that to become apparent because our traditional value system survived intact for such a long time. . . . Without a value system it is going to be very difficult to maintain high standards in our society. . . . The failure to rally around a set of values means that universities are turning out potentially highly skilled barbarians.

—*U.S. News and World Report*,
November 10, 1980

President Franklin Delano Roosevelt: [To] train a man in mind and not in morals is to train a menace to society.

Ted Koppel, Anchor, ABC *Nightline*: We have actually convinced ourselves that slogans will save us. Shoot-up if you must, but use a clean needle. Enjoy sex whenever and with whomever you wish, but wear a condom. No! The answer is no. Not because it isn't cool or smart or because you might end up in jail or dying in an AIDS ward, but no because it's wrong, because we have spent 5000 years as a race of rational human beings, trying to drag ourselves out of the primeval slime by searching for truth and moral absolutes in their purest form. Truth is not a polite tap on the shoulder—it is a howling reproach. What Moses brought down from Mount Sinai were not the Ten Suggestions.

> —Commencement address to the Class
> of 1987 at Duke University,
> Durham, North Carolina

Dr. C. Everett Koop, Surgeon General: I don't think sex education should be taught value-free. I think if you try to teach sex education value-free, what you are teaching is sexual technique. It's like teaching a 13-year-old boy how to drive a car. You get him all enthusiastic and then you say, "Now you can't do this until you're 18." That's not right. When you teach children sexual technique without responsibility and morality, they will do what the car driver does and go out and drive.

> —Liberty Report, March 1987

Appendix B

God's Ten Values

God gave the Ten Commandments to Moses (see Exodus 20:3–17). They are still of value to our generation. In fact, they will always be "God's Ten Values."

Value #1 *God*	You shall have no other Gods before me (v. 3).
Value #2 *God's Character*	You shall not make for yourself an idol in the form of anything in heaven above or on the earth beneath or in the waters below. You shall not bow down to them or worship them; for I, the LORD your God, am a jealous God, punishing the children for the sin of the fathers to the third and fourth generation of those who hate me, but showing love to thousands who love me and keep my commandments (vv. 4–6).
Value #3 *God's Name*	You shall not misuse the name of the LORD your God, for the LORD will not hold anyone guiltless who misuses his name (v. 7).
Value #4 *God's Day*	Remember the Sabbath day by keeping it holy. Six days you shall

labor and do all your work, but the seventh day is a Sabbath to the LORD your God. On it you shall not do any work, neither you, nor your son or daughter, nor your man-servant or maidservant, nor your animals, nor the alien within your gates. For in six days the LORD made the heavens and the earth, the sea, and all that is in them, but he rested on the seventh day. Therefore the LORD blessed the Sabbath day and made it holy (vv. 8–11).

Value #5
Parents

Honor your father and your mother, so that you may live long in the land the LORD your God is giving you (v. 12).

Value #6
Human Life

You shall not murder (v. 13).

Value #7
Moral Purity

You shall not commit adultery (v. 14).

Value #8
Private Property

You shall not steal (v. 15).

Value #9
Truth and Integrity

You shall not give false testimony against your neighbor (v. 16).

Value #10
Eternal Value System

You shall not covet your neighbor's house. You shall not covet your neighbor's wife, or his manservant or maidservant, his ox or donkey, or anything that belongs to your neighbor (v. 17).